I HELD THE HAND OF JESUS IN HEAVEN

MIKE McKINSEY

Peak View Press
An Imprint for GracePoint Publishing
(www.GracePointPublishing.com)

PEAK VIEW
— PRESS —

GracePoint Matrix, LLC
624 S. Cascade Ave, Suite 201, Colorado Springs, CO 80903
www.GracePointMatrix.com Email: Admin@GracePointMatrix.com
SAN # 991-6032

A Library of Congress Control Number has been requested and is pending.
ISBN: 978-1-968891-87-9
eISBN: 978-1-968891-89-3

Books may be purchased for educational, business, or sales promotional use
For non-retail bulk order requests contact Orders@GracePointPublishing.com

To my wife, Melissa, who taught me what it's like to be truly loved. To my children whose love and dedication have never wavered. To my friends, especially those who supported me in the valleys. To the courageous followers of Christ, scattered, silenced, and suffering in shadows, yet unwavering in faith: This book is dedicated to you

OTHER BOOKS BY MIKE McKINSEY

Accidental Heaven

Death is like moving.
I'm not thrilled about the process,
but I'm looking forward to the destination.

Mike McKinsey

In my Father's house are many mansions. And one of them is mine!

Mike McKinsey

TABLE OF CONTENTS

PREFACE

Shortly after my near-death experience (NDE), I was consumed by an unquenchable thirst to explore NDEs, Heaven and the mysteries of the afterlife. I was reading a book called *Heaven* by Randy Alcorn. In it, he was describing the "intermediate" or "transitional" Heaven as being a physical place right now. I had never thought of Heaven like that, but Randy told the story of Stephen in the Bible; as he was being stoned to death, he saw Heaven opened up. Stephen described seeing Jesus standing at the right hand of the Father. Randy goes on to say that what Stephen saw was a physical attribute of Jesus. Stephen didn't see Jesus floating or describe him as a spirit or ghost; he saw the physical person of Jesus, standing.

There are other clues in the Bible as well that lead me to believe in a physical, intermediate Heaven. In the parable of the rich man and Lazarus, found in Luke 16:19, Jesus describes two distinct places after death, a place of comfort, often interpreted as the intermediate Heaven where Lazarus is taken, and a place of torment where the rich man goes. This parable implies that there's a real physical existence after death.

"There was a rich man who was dressed in purple and fine linen and lived in luxury every day. At his gate was laid a beggar named Lazarus, covered with sores and longing to eat what fell from the rich man's table. Even the dogs came and licked his sores. The time came when the beggar died and the angels carried him to Abraham's side. The rich man also died and was buried. In Hades, where he was in torment, he looked up and saw Abraham far away, with Lazarus by his side. So he called to him, 'Father Abraham, have pity on me and send Lazarus to dip the tip of his finger in water and cool my tongue, because I am in agony in this fire.' But Abraham replied, 'Son, remember that in your lifetime you received your good things, while Lazarus received bad things, but now he is comforted here and you are in agony. And besides all this, between us and you, a great chasm has been set in place, so that those who want to go from here to you cannot, nor can anyone cross over from there to us.' He answered, 'Then I beg you, father, send Lazarus to my family, for I have five brothers. Let him warn them, so that they will not also come to this place of torment.' Abraham replied, 'They have Moses and the Prophets; let them listen to them.' 'No, father Abraham,' he said, 'but if someone from the dead goes to them, they will repent.' He said to him, 'If they do not listen to Moses and the Prophets, they will not be convinced even if someone rises from the dead.'"

In Revelation 6:9–11 John sees the souls of those who have been slain because of the Word of God and the testimony they had maintained. They are described as being under the altar in Heaven, crying out for justice. This suggests that believers who have died are conscious and present in a specific location in Heaven. It also suggests that they are aware of time and wearing white robes, another physical attribute.

"When he opened the fifth seal, I saw under the altar the souls of those who had been slain because of the word of God and the testimony they had maintained. They called out in a loud voice, 'How long, Sovereign Lord, holy and true, until you judge the inhabitants of the earth and avenge our blood?' Then each of them was given a white robe, and they were told to wait a little longer, until the full number of their fellow servants, their brothers and sisters, were killed just as they had been."

In Acts 1:9–11, after his resurrection, Jesus ascends into Heaven in a physical body. The angels tell the disciples, "The same Jesus who has been taken from you into heaven will come back in the same way you have seen him go into heaven." This implies that Heaven is a physical place, where Jesus resides in his glorified body.

"After he said this, he was taken up before their very eyes, and a cloud hid him from their sight. They were looking intently up into the sky, when suddenly two men dressed in white stood beside them. 'Men of Galilee,' they said, 'why do you stand here looking into the sky? This same Jesus, who has been taken from you into heaven, will come back in the same way you have seen him go into heaven.'"

In Revelation 7:9–17 John describes a great multitude standing before the throne of God worshiping Him. This scene includes physical elements like robes, palm branches, and the throne itself, suggesting a tangible physical reality in Heaven.

"After this I looked, and there before me was a great multitude that no one could count, from every nation, tribe, people, and language, standing before the throne and before the Lamb. They were wearing white robes and were holding palm branches in their hands. And they cried out in a loud voice: 'Salvation belongs to our God, who sits on the throne, and to the Lamb.' All the angels were standing around the throne and around the elders and the four living creatures. They fell down on their faces before the throne and worshiped God, 12 saying: 'Amen! Praise and glory and wisdom and thanks and honor and power and strength be to our God for ever and ever. Amen!' Then one of the elders asked me, 'These in white robes—who are they, and where did they come from?' I answered, 'Sir, you know.' And he said, 'These are they who have come out of the great tribulation; they have washed their robes and made them white in the blood of the Lamb. Therefore, they are before the throne of God and serve him day and night in his temple; and he who sits on the throne will shelter them with his presence. Never again will they hunger; never again will they thirst. The sun will not beat down on them, nor any scorching heat. For the Lamb at the center of the throne will be their shepherd; he will lead them to springs of living water. And God will wipe away every tear from their eyes.'"

It was in the moment of reading the story of Stephen that the idea for my first book flooded into my mind. It was as if God told me, "Here is the story I want you to write and now is the time!"

So I started writing *Accidental Heaven*, which was inspired by the near-death experience I had a few years prior. I wrote that book as a fictional novel because I wanted to explore the fun fact that Heaven, the intermediate Heaven that is, could actually be a real, physical place out there somewhere. After all, I wrote, "Couldn't God put Heaven out there somewhere and just hide out from us? Of course He could; He's God!"

Now, I realize I may have introduced some of you to a new term, that being, "intermediate Heaven." The apostle Paul puts it this way in 1 Thessalonians 4:17: "After that, we who are still alive and are left will be caught up together with them in the clouds to meet the Lord in the air. And so we will be with the Lord forever." The Bible also gives us clues as to what happens to us when we die. In 2 Corinthians 5:8, the apostle Paul writes, "We are confident, I say, and willing rather to be absent from the body, and to be present with the Lord." The expression absent from the body refers to physical death. When this life ends, believers will be immediately ushered into the glorious presence of the Lord. Then we will see Him face-to-face (1 Corinthians 13:12). And, at that moment, we will be "present with the Lord." So the intermediate Heaven is just that. It's our temporary home until God remakes the earth, removes the curse of sin and comes to dwell with us forever.

God tells us in Revelation 21:1 that Heaven will change. John says, "Then I saw a new heaven and a new earth, for the first earth had passed away, and there was no longer any sea. I saw the Holy City, the new Jerusalem, coming down out of heaven from God, prepared as a bride beautifully dressed for her husband. And I heard a loud voice from the throne saying, 'Look! God's dwelling place is now among the people, and he will dwell with them. They will be his people, and God himself will be with them and be their God.'" (I believe that is the city I was shown by Jesus in my near-death experience.)

Granted, I am not a writer, as I said in the preface of *Accidental Heaven*, so writing my first novel took a long time. It actually took eight years to complete! But when it was finished, I felt like God was happy with my work. There were days when I would sit down at my desk and write and get so lost in thought and in the momentum of writing that time just flew. There were a few times when I realized I had been writing for four or five hours straight and I would have to go back and read to know what I had written! I knew the Holy Spirit was helping me write and there were moments when He just took over!

By that time I had already gone through a divorce and gotten remarried. In doing so, it was as if God had written the last chapter of my book. God told me to write about my NDE and my Jesus encounter, but He did not tell me that I could say what happened on the second day in the hospital yet. I had to wait until He told me that the time was right to tell that part of the story.

You see, when I told the story of my near-death experience to a couple of my friends, they would hang onto every word. They would cry with me as I told of how Jesus took me to Heaven and showed me His glory. My description of what I saw and felt had everyone completely mezmerized. But their expressions changed as I told them about the next day, how Jesus showed up again and spoke to me in the hospital room. And it wasn't just one person; it was everyone. Although, when I say everyone, I mean about a dozen of my closest friends, including my wife. When I got to the three-hour conversation that I had with Jesus, their expressions changed from "Wow!" to "Okay, you're crazy!" So I just learned to stop telling that part of the story. That was my realization that God wanted me to hold off on telling that portion of my hospital stay. For the time being.

I believe God was preparing me for the battle that was to come to convince people to believe. And I wasn't the only one He was preparing. He was also preparing the world. The timing just wasn't right. I pictured the disciples back in the day trying to convince people that Jesus had risen from the grave. People have a hard time believing stuff like that. It's not like those things happen every day. He would tell me when that time was. So, about ten years later, Guideposts contacted me about my NDE story, and they printed it in their *Witnessing Heaven* series, in the book entitled *Glimpses of Eternity*.

As a result of that publication, I began a marketing tour talking about my NDE and the Guideposts story. This was now twenty years after my NDE and YouTube had become a very popular platform for sharing experiences like mine, and there were actually channels that featured nothing but NDEs. At the time of my NDE, YouTube was mostly music videos!

A year later, after I made all these YouTube appearances, God told me, "Now is the time to tell the rest of the story," and He wanted me to write my current book.

I was actually reading a comment from someone that said, "Your high temperature caused a hallucination." I knew that my temperature couldn't be the factor because, the next day, Jesus was talking to me at the very moment a nurse checked my temperature and it was almost normal.

It was at that moment of reading that particular comment that I heard God say, "Now is the time. You must tell the rest of the story. We know the truth. You are ready and the world will be more receptive. I have prepared you for this task, so go now and tell the full story. Hold nothing back. I will be with you. Now is the time."

So this book is a testament to the profound and transformative encounter I experienced during what I can only describe as the most challenging and enlightening twelve days of my life. It is a story of pain, fear, and uncertainty, but more importantly, it is a story of hope, redemption, and divine love from my savior.

In the sterile, fluorescent-lit corridors of a hospital, I found myself teetering on the edge of life and death. It was during that time, in the midst of my deepest despair and vulnerability, that I encountered Jesus in a way that defies human explanation. This was a very physical encounter with Jesus that gave me a profound sense of peace, presence, and unconditional love that transcended my understanding.

This book is my attempt to share that experience with you. It is not just a recounting of events but a journey into the depths of faith, the power of divine intervention, and the incredible ways in which God can use even our darkest moments to reveal His light. It is a story of how, in the midst of suffering, I found a renewed sense of purpose and a deeper connection to Jesus. This is my love story with my savior and the account of the beginning of my relationship with Him.

CHAPTER 1
GROWING UP

I was raised in Lodi, California, the Zinfandel capital of the world! We lived about twenty miles from town, but our little neighborhood was rather unique. Our street was located out in the country, completely isolated from any other neighborhood, and had about fifteen houses on it. Each house had a couple acres and when we moved in, all the houses were brand-new. There were lots of young families so I always had friends to play with.

One of my favorite memories of growing up there was our Fourth of July celebration. All the men in the neighborhood got together the day before and dug a big pit. Then they wrapped up a pig in wet banana leaves and burlap sackcloth, dropped it in the pit onto hot coals and covered it with more hot coals and lava rocks, and then buried it. They let that pig cook underground all night, Hawaiian style. On the Fourth, all the neighbors met and had a giant luau. Every family brought their favorite picnic side dishes to complement the star of the show, the cooked pig! It was a great time. And then, when the sun went down, we had our own private fireworks show. I loved growing up in the country!

My mom moved to America from Holland with her family when she was sixteen years old. Her father was a registered nurse in Holland and owned a rest home. Mom had lots of crazy stories about the Nazis during the war, although we had to pry the stories out of her. One story she loved telling, though, was how dumb they were because the Nazi troops wore heavy boots, so everyone knew when they were coming because the boots echoed off the brick streets. This was important because my grandfather, Grampa Ben, hid Jews from the Nazis between the floors of the nursing home. I always wished I had explored that story with Mom when I got older, but that was about the extent of any conversation about the war. As it is with many people who live through a war, they don't like talking about it.

My mother was a stay-at-home mom until I went to high school. She must have figured that by the time I started the ninth grade I was old enough to ride the bus home and take care of myself until she got home from work. She took a job at a bank and worked there until she finally retired.

Mom had a big personality and was always the life of the party everywhere she went. Even though she came to America as a teenager, she had no accent whatsoever! Her English was perfect. But she struggled every once in a while with pronunciations. One of the funniest examples of this was when we were camping at Calaveras Big Trees State Park. We were walking on one of the back roads through the park and mom saw a rock that looked like a tortoise. She stopped all the kids and said, "Oh look at that," while pointing at the rock. "It looks like a tor-toys!" We all laughed and explained how to actually pronounce tortoise. She had seen the word in writing but had never heard it pronounced. Needless to say, that moment became legendary in my family! And Mom took it all in stride, which was typical of her personality. She could always laugh at herself.

My father was a deputy sheriff for San Joaquin County and was on patrol for a few years before moving into the technical services department doing forensic stuff such as fingerprints and facial recognition with slides. Dad was trained by the FBI in Washington, DC, and became quite a fingerprint expert. Today, I tell people that Dad was CSI before CSI was cool!

My dad taught me a lot of typical father/son kinds of things, like how to hunt and fish. We even tried backpacking, but only once, mostly because of the outcome! We drove up past our usual camping spot near Dorrington, California, one weekend. A few of my dad's work buddies had told him about a fishing spot, but you had to hike to it about five miles in and five miles back out. So we decided to give it a try. I had been getting pretty interested in backpacking anyway, so Dad figured this would be a great opportunity to give it a try. Five miles each way isn't that far!

So we drove to the spot where his friends had told him to park, loaded up our packs and started walking. You have to remember, this was way before GPS, or Google Maps, or any sort of tracking devices. Back then, you looked at a map and just started! There was unfortunately no trail, so we were just walking in the direction of the lake. What Dad's friends had failed to mention were all the elevation changes. We started walking up a large hill. I figured once we got to the top of that hill, we would start walking down, but no such luck. There was another, even bigger hill to climb after that first one. The ground eventually leveled out a bit, but it seemed like it was all uphill.

Well, we walked for a few hours, stopping every once in a while to catch our breath. But we kept going. We walked and walked and walked. We would go to the highest point we could find and look around for the elusive lake, but we never saw it. After about four hours, we decided to head back to the car. We actually got back to the car pretty quickly, since the way back was mostly downhill! We decided we would go back to our favorite campground and spend the night and go fishing the next morning in one of the rivers within the State Park. We got there just before sundown and, luckily, they had some open camping spaces. But we had to take a campsite in one of the south campgrounds, which were much more remote than the sites in the north.

So we made a campfire, cooked our dinner and decided to go to sleep early. We were both exhausted. We didn't have a tent, since we didn't want to pack in the extra weight on our backpacking trip, so we decided to sleep in the back of the station wagon. We got the sleeping bags laid out in the back, but just before crawling in I told Dad I had to use the restroom.

The campground had bathrooms, but the closest one was about a quarter mile from the car, so I decided to use one of the trees nearby! I grabbed the flashlight, walked a few feet from the car and heard a loud crash, like metal being thrown onto the street. I jumped back in the car and yelled at my dad, "There's a bear out there!"

Dad said, "There are no bears here," and tried to calm me down.

With a little more encouragement, I decided to try again. So I stepped out again, but this time I walked a little further before shining the flashlight across the street. That's when I saw it. I was standing about six feet from the biggest brown bear I had ever seen! He was rummaging through one of the trash cans across the road and happened to stand up on his hind legs as he turned to look at me. I screamed like a little girl and jumped back in the car. I took the flashlight and pointed it through the window as I was telling Dad that there was, in fact, a giant bear! Dad admitted that he was wrong the first time! So we watched the bear finish his dinner of garbage scraps, and he finally left on all fours. Needless to say, I didn't have to go to the bathroom anymore.

The next day, after a fun morning of fishing, we told one of the rangers about the bear incident. He said, "Oh, that's old Hercules. He's been here for years and never hurts anyone. He just comes to the camp at night for snacks."

We always camped there during the summers, but never saw Hercules again. A few years after that incident, the park started installing bear-proof garbage containers.

And just another note about our backpacking trip. I looked up Wheeler Lake about forty years after our attempt to hike there. There is now a paved road that goes all the way in. I wish my dad could have lived long enough to see that. It would have been fun to go back there with him, but I'm sure the fishing wouldn't be as legendary as it supposedly was before the road.

CHAPTER 2
SETTING THE STAGE

When I was a young kid, my grandfather passed away. He was Catholic and had a funeral at a very large cathedral. I was amazed at how big and fancy the church was. I believe it was my first time in such a spectacular church. I was struck by the majesty of it. I remember sitting there as the priest was up on the altar swinging a metal ball back and forth. The ball had holes and there was smoke coming out of them. If you want to get the attention of a little kid, use smoke or fire! It was at that moment that I sat up and actually started paying attention! The priest started talking about my grandfather. He said, "Pete is in a better place now. A place where there is no pain, no sorrow, and no tears."

I thought to myself, *That sounds like a really cool place.* Right then and there, I asked God to show me Heaven. That request became a nightly prayer for a really long time for me. My prayers went something like, "Now I lay me down to sleep, I pray the Lord my soul to keep. If I should die before I wake, I pray the Lord my soul to take. Oh, and one more thing, God; can you show me Heaven?"

Looking back on that prayer, it was simple and probably didn't mean a lot to a little kid, except for the "show me Heaven" part. I was serious. I wanted to see it. And, quite frankly, I didn't think through what I was asking for. I certainly didn't want to die, but I still wanted to see it! Little did I know that, in about forty years, God would answer my childhood prayer.

Showing me Heaven wasn't my only childhood prayer. I had always been captivated by the phrase, "the Glory of the Lord." As a child, I had watched the cartoon *A Charlie Brown Christmas* every year during the holidays. Back then, you couldn't stream a show and watch whenever you wanted. You had to gather around the television at a certain time on a certain night if you wanted to see the show. And you waited for commercial breaks to grab snacks or use the restroom! It's amazing how things have changed!

In the Charlie Brown special, Linus had a part where he walked out on stage and said, "The glory of the Lord shone all around them." It's actually a passage from the Bible and is found in Luke 2:9. *"And an angel of the Lord appeared to them, and the glory of the Lord shone all around them, and they were terrified."*

It had always brought tears to my young eyes. As a child I had wondered, *If this was the Lord God, creator of Heaven and Earth, what must His glory be like?* That whole passage is pretty amazing. It also talks about angels appearing and talks about the heavenly host. Wow! I remember praying to God as a child, asking Him to show me His glory. And just like my prayer of showing me Heaven, this became a second request I made over and over to the Lord. Show me Heaven and show me your glory.

I've always believed in God. As I grew up, however, I fell into a life of just playing Christian. I would call myself a "Sunday Christian." I went to church every now and then and certainly enjoyed it, but it didn't stick with me during the week. I wasn't living for Christ or His Kingdom. But I still had faith. When I was a teenager, my dad started going to church with us. I think it was more because his schedule had changed and he now had weekends off. Mom always took me and my two sisters to the big Presbyterian church downtown. But when we moved to the country, we joined a Lutheran church.

I became very involved in the youth group there and loved it. We had meetings on Sunday nights with a little bit of Bible study and lots of playtime. I played guitar for the group and every once in a while I got to play in church. Oh, the life of a budding musician. I wish I had kept playing, but as I grew up, got married, and kids started to dominate my life, my dedication to keep playing guitar took the inevitable back seat. Believe me when I say I have no regrets. I love my kids. I have four children—Ben, Hilary, Chris, and Jake. I had my first son at the ripe old age of twenty! But I wouldn't change a thing. My family meant the world to me and they still do.

When we bought our first home, we lived next door to some very devoted Christians, Cindy and Will. As we got to know them better, they invited us to their church. It was a small church, but I really liked it. We even started doing a Bible study with them separate from church. After the last night of our Bible studies, Cindy asked if I wanted to get baptized. During the Bible study, we learned about salvation. I had heard all this stuff before, but for some reason, I thought that my confirmation class at the Lutheran church was good enough to get me into Heaven. But because of that Bible study with Cindy and Will, I learned that you need to accept the free gift of everlasting life offered by Jesus. And as an outward sign to the world, you needed to get baptized.

When I told Cindy that I would love to get baptized, she said, "Let's go!"

I said, "Now?" This was about nine o'clock at night! "Isn't the church closed?" I asked.

Cindy smiled and said, "Yes, but we have keys." So off we went to the church.

Will opened the church and went straight to the back where the dunking tub was and started filling it up with warm water. When it was full, we put on some gowns and waded in. Will baptized me that night. Cindy baptized my wife. The date was May 30, 1989. That's the day I was officially adopted into the family of Jesus. And I will know Cindy and Will forever!

As I said earlier, even after being baptized and professing my faith to the world, I fell into the trap of continuing life as a Sunday Christian.

Here's what I mean by living as a "Sunday Christian," a way of life that I think describes a lot of people out there, even the ones active in church. It refers to the practice of outwardly expressing your faith and religious devotion primarily on Sundays, particularly during church services, while largely neglecting spiritual practices and moral principles during the rest of the week. I've always been told that a church is a hospital for sinners. The term Sunday Christian is often used critically to describe individuals who compartmentalize their faith, treating it as a weekly ritual rather than a guiding force in their daily lives. For many, this lifestyle can stem from a desire to maintain a sense of religious identity or social belonging without fully committing to the transformative aspects of their faith.

While attending church on Sundays may provide a sense of community and spiritual refreshment, the lack of integration of faith into everyday life can lead to a shallow or inconsistent spiritual experience.

The concern about living as a Sunday Christian lies in the disconnect between belief and action. Faith, in many religious traditions, is meant to be a holistic commitment that influences one's thoughts, decisions, and interactions with others. When faith is confined to a single day of the week, it risks becoming performative rather than transformative. For example, a Sunday Christian might participate in worship, recite prayers, and listen to sermons but fail to extend kindness, honesty, or forgiveness in their personal and professional lives. This inconsistency can lead to a sense of emptiness or hypocrisy as the individual may feel they are not truly living out the values they profess to believe. And I hate hypocrites, but I failed to identify that trait in my own personality. I never considered myself unkind to anyone, but I lived life with a pretty cynical view of society.

Breaking free from the Sunday Christian mindset requires intentional effort to integrate faith into every aspect of life. This might involve daily prayer or meditation, regular reflection on religious teachings, and a conscious effort to align one's actions with one's beliefs. It also means seeking opportunities to serve others, practice humility, and cultivate a genuine relationship with the divine beyond the walls of a church. By doing so, faith becomes a lived experience rather than a weekly obligation, fostering deeper spiritual growth and a more authentic connection to one's religious community. Ultimately, living out one's faith consistently can lead to a more meaningful and fulfilling spiritual journey.

CHAPTER 3
VENTURA

It was a beautiful setting for a wedding, but Ventura, California, rarely disappoints. My oldest son had attended college in Santa Barbara for a few years. He had graduated and gotten a job at a small clinic as a nuclear medicine technologist. To say he had an amazing future ahead of him was an understatement. He had met a beautiful young lady in church a few years prior. She was perfect for my son. She was a stunning girl with red hair and bright blue eyes and very athletic, a perfect match for him. Her parents had lived in Ventura for about ten years. They had a beautiful home at the top of a hill, overlooking the city and the Pacific Ocean. The couple had decided to have their wedding there, close to the bride's family, and my wife and I happily agreed.

At that time, we were living about five hours north in the little town of Manteca. We had gotten to Ventura the Wednesday before after deciding to make this event a mini vacation. It was, after all, the last weekend of summer before my three younger kids started back to school.

We checked into the hotel in the afternoon. It was a really nice, mission-style hotel that had been completely renovated a few years prior to our stay. It was one of those large properties with lots of trees and meandering paths under wisteria and other pretty hanging vines. Along all the paths were benches and little private sitting areas, perfect for tucking in with a good book!

My son's bride-to-be had booked a block of rooms for all the out-of-town guests. Most of those guests were set to arrive on Thursday night or Friday. When we were checking in, my younger sons noticed a very large park connected to the hotel property and asked if they could go play some home run derby. Baseball is very important in my family. All three of my boys played organized ball from age five! They all loved the game and they were really good! I coached all of them at some point in their amateur careers. Looking back, baseball was the glue that held my family together. We always supported one another and attended every game all the kids played. Many times our involvement was not only coaching but also keeping score, umpiring, or just sitting in the stands with the other parents, all while solving the world's problems! We spent a lot of time at the ball fields and I loved every minute of it.

After a few trips to the car, I had all the bags safely stored in the room. As soon as the last suitcase was stashed away, the two boys ran off to the park with their Wiffle balls and bats.

"They still love playing baseball, don't they?" asked my wife as the boys sped past.

"It's who we are," I said. It was true. I asked my wife and daughter, "Are you guys coming?"

My daughter looked at my wife and answered for both of them. "We wouldn't miss it for the world."

When we got to the park, the boys started clapping. They had already decided what imaginary line was going to be the home run "fence." All the rules were in place and all I had to do was join in. That was just the way I liked it. I decided to do a little stretching, just to send a message to the boys that I was taking this little game of theirs very seriously. It's probably a good time to let you know that we are a very competitive family. But it's always in good fun.

My youngest son shouted at me, "Hey Dad, you're up!" I grabbed the big yellow plastic bat and stepped into the imaginary batter's box. "What's a home run again?" I asked.

One of the boys yelled from about a hundred feet away. "Just over my head, past these two trees!" He spread his arms apart and pointed at a couple of trees on each side of him.

"That seems kind of far doesn't it?" I was looking for some small advantage in this game. After all, I was playing with kids twenty years my junior, and I hadn't swung a baseball bat in quite a while. It was only a plastic bat, but I figured it was worth getting some sort of consolation.

"It's not that far!" they both yelled back in unison. Both the boys looked at each other and laughed.

My daughter had opted out of playing baseball, so it was just me and my two sons, Chris and Jake. Jake is my youngest and he was pitching. He didn't give me any time to reply; he wound up and threw the little plastic ball. It whistled past my face.

"Strike," came the call from Jake.

"You call that a strike? That ball was two feet outside!" I knew I didn't have a chance at getting a strike call overturned, but I wanted to reiterate that I poured my full effort into every aspect of the game.

"Come on, Dad, everyone gets ten swings. You can't strike out! What's the point in arguing?" Jake laughed.

"Okay, okay," I said. I stepped out of the imaginary batter's box, and spit on my hands and rubbed them together. I dug my feet into the grass and raised my arms for the next swing. "That's more like it!"

I swung at the next pitch and sent the ball sailing over Chris's head for a home run.

He turned and yelled back as he ran toward the ball, "I told you it wasn't that far!"

I laughed as I watched my son run to retrieve the ball, realizing that the game wouldn't be as hard as I had thought.

The game went on for about an hour. We had fun swinging the bat and chasing balls as my wife and daughter sat and watched from a blanket in the shade. Every once in a while my daughter would shoot a few pictures of all of us in our element. Finally, exhausted, I called the boys together.

"Guys, this was a lot of fun, but we better clean up and get ready for dinner. We're meeting everyone at a little restaurant downtown in a couple hours."

My wife gave me a hug. "You did great. I'm proud of you, keeping up with those youngsters."

❖ ❖ ❖

I got out of the shower, rubbed my stomach and thought, *I don't feel too good. Oh no, not now! Am I getting the flu?* I asked my wife if she felt alright, thinking it might have been something we ate. "I'm fine," she said. "Could it be from the baseball this afternoon? You're not as young as you used to be, you know! And you did try awfully hard to beat those youngsters. I know how competitive you guys are." She came over and put her palm on my forehead. "No fever." She looked concerned, though. "Our son is getting married in two days, Mike. You've got a lot to do between now and then. Do you think you'll be alright?"

I shrugged my shoulders and held the back of my own hand up to my forehead. "I don't know. I don't think I have a fever. But my stomach. Ouch!" I suddenly felt awful but knew that I had to keep it together for a couple more days. "I'm sure I can take something and I'll be fine. It just feels like the flu or something. I'll just put off being sick until we get home." I buttoned up my shirt. "Did we bring any Tylenol?"

❖ ❖ ❖

We spent Thursday with my son's future in-laws in the little beach town of Ventura, getting to know them better. We found a cute little breakfast spot near the beach that served giant cinnamon rolls, and they had room for all of us! We spent the rest of the morning shopping before deciding on grabbing sandwiches and heading to the beach for an impromptu picnic. I was surprisingly hungry considering the nagging flu that had harassed me the night before.

Summers on the California coast are usually blanketed in fog and today was no exception. We grabbed a bunch of sandwiches in a little sub shop and walked towards the beach. As we stepped onto the sand, the sun broke out and the fog quickly dissipated. The sun quickly warmed and the bright rays reflected off the wet sand as I surveyed the rocky coastline for the perfect spot. Nine hungry mouths to feed and a beach full of promising, yet ultimately disappointing, lunch spots. My boys already had sand all over them after running ahead of the group and doing what boys do at the beach! As they ran after each other, a cloud of sand followed in their wake. They were halfway to the water, leaving me to navigate the logistical nightmare of a group picnic. This small beach town, usually so charming, felt like a battlefield today. Every potential spot was either too crowded, too exposed, or simply lacked the crucial element: enough space for nine people plus all the para-phernalia of a family lunch. I felt a bead of sweat trickle down my temple; this was turning into less of a beach day and more of an expedition.

Then a glint of something unexpected caught my eye—a small, secluded cove nestled behind a rocky outcrop. It wasn't marked on any map, a hidden gem only discoverable by those who ventured past the main beach. The cove itself was small, but surprisingly sheltered, with a natural rock wall forming a windbreak. A small, sandy area offered enough space to lay out our blankets and, best of all, it offered a breathtaking view of the ocean—a panoramic vista of waves crashing against the cliffs. The only other occupants were a family of seagulls, serenely perched on a nearby rock. The kids, initially disappointed by the trek, erupted in cheers when they saw the cove's beauty. It was perfect.

We spread out our feast—sandwiches, chips, and sodas—a colorful array on the soft sand. The kids ran, played, and shrieked with delight, their laughter echoing off the rocks. As I watched them, the sun warming my face, I realized this wasn't just about finding a lunch spot; it was about finding a place of peace and unexpected beauty, a secret sanctuary hidden in plain sight. The perfect spot for a family lunch, away from the crowds, a memory made more valuable by the journey of discovering it. That hidden cove, found in the midst of a frantic search, became more than just a place to eat; it was a symbol of the adventure of family and the joy of unexpected discoveries.

CHAPTER 4
REHEARSAL DINNER

Ben tapped his knife on the side of his glass of water. "Ting, ting, ting, ting." He stood up and looked around at all his family and close friends. He had their full attention; everyone in the room looked at him, anticipating a speech.

"Mawage!" he said in his best impression of *The Princess Bride*'s priest. Suddenly the quiet room was filled with laughter. Ben always knew how to entertain a large group of people. Ever since he was a little boy, barely able to walk, he had been the entertainer of the family. It wasn't unusual for Ben, while running around in his diapers, to summersault clumsily and wait for a reaction. He usually got the response he was looking for.

But it hadn't always been fun and games. Once, when Ben was a little over a year old, my wife and I had been eating dinner with my wife's mother. It was just the three of us and baby Ben, in his high chair, sitting around the kitchen table. During a lull in the conversation, Ben yelled out, "Fudge!" only, just like Ralphie in *A Christmas Story*, he didn't say fudge! He blurted out the real fword! We all let out a loud and collective gasp, which caused Ben to drop his head onto the high chair tray and start to cry. I couldn't help but laugh, which brought a few jeers from my wife.

Today, though, he was pleasing the crowd. He looked around the room again with a big smile and laughed right along with all the dinner guests.

"I told my dad I was going to have the preacher start the ceremony tomorrow by saying that. As you may or may not know, that's a line from the movie *The Princess Bride*. It's one of our favorite movies—well, everyone except my mom! She hates it when we quote movies, but we all get a kick out of it. But seriously, it is marriage that brings us together today."

Chris, who was sitting next to Ben, was shaking his head and giggling. He said quietly, "I can't believe you said that."

Ben looked at his younger brother and winked, then looked back out at the crowd. Some of them were still chuckling and shaking their heads. "This rehearsal dinner is just the beginning of our celebration. I wanted to say thank you to everyone for coming all this way to see us get hitched. Believe it or not, we take this very seriously. Tomorrow is going to be the most important day in our lives. Heather and I are so happy you all found a way to share this day with us. We love you all. I would like to ask my dad to lead us in prayer before we eat." Ben looked toward me as a few waiters entered the room carrying the entrées. They stopped when they saw the crowd was about to pray.

"Dad, would you mind?" Ben tried to catch my eye from across the room but paused when he saw my face. "Dad, are you okay? You don't look so good."

I nodded, although I agreed with my son. In fact, I was feeling worse by the minute and I was struggling to keep it together. Now wasn't the time to let my family down.

"I'm okay. We played a little home run derby a couple days ago and it took a lot out of your old man. Actually, I think I might be coming down with the flu. Maybe I can have the preacher lay hands on me tomorrow before the ceremony!" Everyone in the banquet room laughed, including the waiters.

I waited for the laughter to die down then started. "Let's bow our heads and pray." I led my family and friends in a prayer and asked God for blessings on the family and on Ben's marriage and new life. As I did, I could feel my stomach churning and growling. I was sure that everyone in the room could hear it but tried to put it to the side. I didn't have time to get sick right now.

❖ ❖ ❖

Later that night, everyone went back to the hotel. My son and I sat in the hotel bar: Ben was sipping a martini and I was clutching a glass of wine but knew I should have stuck with water. We spent the last few minutes of the evening alone talking about how much fun tomorrow would bring. It was Ben's last evening as a single man, and we both relished the last few minutes of a long day together in peace and quiet.

"You better get up to bed, Ben," I finally said as we reached the bottom of our glasses. "You have a really big day ahead of you."

"That's a good idea, Dad. Thanks for everything. I hope you feel better in the morning." Ben hugged me and turned and walked to the elevator.

I sat back down for a minute and wondered if a good night's sleep was all I needed. Maybe the stress of having my first son get married was making me ill. My stomach churned, though, disagreeing with this easy diagnosis. There had to be more to it than stress, I thought. I had always handled stress pretty well; my job was extremely stressful, but it never made me sick and I couldn't remember ever having felt this bad before. My stomach physically hurt and I was starting to sweat. I was sure I had a fever. *It's got to be the flu, but this is a nasty one,* I thought. I finally walked up the stairs to my room. *What a great day,* I thought. *So good.*

"Still feeling sick?" my wife asked as I entered the room. I bent over to try to alleviate the pain that was now welling up inside my abdomen. "I feel terrible! This isn't good... maybe I'm just all backed up. Come to think of it I haven't gone to the bathroom, number two, since we got here. That's not normal, is it?"

"TMI," my wife quipped back with a bit of irreverence. "Traveling can do that sometimes, but we're not that far from home."

I rubbed my eyes, grimacing in pain as I watched my wife turn over under the covers. "I think I'll go get some pink stuff. They have Quick Stops down here, right?"

"Mike, maybe we should go get you checked out. There's bound to be a hospital around here somewhere. Something could be seriously wrong!"

I shook my head. "It's not that bad, I'm sure I'm fine. But I think I'm going to go find a store that sells something to soothe the stomach. If that doesn't work, we'll go to a hospital, but not until after the wedding. I'll be right back."

I kissed my wife on the cheek, grabbed my car keys, and left.

❖ ❖ ❖

I drove around downtown Ventura, looking for an all-night Quick Stop market. The only GPS back then was Garmin, but I wasn't fortunate enough to have one, so it took a while. When I saw lights in the distance, I knew relief was nearly at hand and I sighed. I parked the car and looked around the tiny parking lot. To my surprise, it was bustling with action. There had to be twenty-five people just wandering around. Most of them didn't look out of place at all; they looked as though they knew exactly what they were doing there.

This could be what they do every night, I thought. I began to wonder if this was such a good idea though. Although it was only a few blocks from the hotel, it didn't look like the safest place in town and the number of people in the parking lot made me a bit nervous.

But the pain in my gut was not letting up and I needed to get some kind of relief. I got out, locked my car, and headed straight to the medicine aisle, where I grabbed some Tylenol and a bottle of Pepto that promised relief in a couple hours.

"Perfect," I said to myself. I was actually relieved when I finally got back to the hotel. Driving around after midnight is not exactly my thing, especially in a strange town. I went to the bathroom and poured a glass of water. I took a few Tylenol and then swallowed some of the thick, pink medication for my stomach. I drank an entire glass of water to wash it down while reading the directions on the package. "Relief within two hours or overnight; either one would be just fine," I murmured.

I quietly slipped under the covers. I was still really uncomfortable and sweaty. I knew I had a fever and quietly prayed that God would grant me a little rest and the Tylenol would take away the pain. But it wasn't to be. I tossed and turned for another three hours before I finally gave up. It was 5:15 in the morning; the morning of my son's wedding. I got up and headed to the bathroom. "Great," I muttered. My stomach hurt so much that I could barely stand it, and I knew I was facing a long day with no sleep at all.

Then I had a brilliant idea. If I could just throw up, I would feel better. I leaned over the toilet and tried sticking my finger down my throat in an unenthusiastic attempt to make myself gag. It didn't work. My son's wedding was in a few hours and here I was, wide awake, burning up with a fever, and leaning over a hotel toilet trying to puke! Talk about deflating. I was sure it was just the flu, but my wife's words were haunting me now. What if it was something more serious? I didn't know what it could be, but I was sure it wasn't going to be pleasant, not with this much pain. Still, there was nothing to be done now; I had to get through Ben's wedding later, and then I would go to the hospital. I splashed some cold water on my face, went back to bed and tossed and turned a few more hours before everyone else finally woke up.

CHAPTER 5
THE WEDDING

It was an absolutely beautiful day for a wedding. The sun was shining and the forecast called for temperatures in the mid-80s. We arrived at Ventura Golf and Country Club before anyone else. I hadn't slept at all the night before and I was still feeling very sick. I was exhausted, but I was hoping that the tuxedo would somehow mask my discomfort. I had taken so much Tylenol to try to get through the ceremony that I wasn't sure if that was helping or making me feel worse. I was sure about one thing though—I was definitely going to a hospital to get checked out as soon as the reception was over. My ears were ringing, which I attributed to all the Tylenol, and I finally felt that if I tried, I might actually be able to throw up. But today I needed to keep it together and put on a happy face. Today was all about the bride and groom. I didn't want to let any more people know how sick I was.

I walked out to the patio, which overlooked the practice green, and watched a few golfers practice their putting. The aroma of freshly cut grass filled the air. A grounds crew was working on the eighteenth green in the distance.

This place is gorgeous, I thought. They were obviously very meticulous about their grooming. The fairways were bright green and looked to be in perfect condition. It was going to be tough for me to be this close to the game I loved, on such a splendid day, and not be able to play. I had started playing golf when I was eighteen years old, when my college buddies and I would go out and play almost every weekend. I got pretty good at it, but when Ben was born, I just didn't have the time to commit to the game. They said, "If you don't play a minimum of twice a week, you won't get any better," and they were right. But there was a short time, when all three of my boys were young, that I bought them all clubs, some of them "kid clubs," and took them out and taught them the game. It was so much fun to watch my youngest son, Jake, swing his clubs. All the boys got pretty good and we always had fun, but there was something incredible about watching a little guy swing a driver and watch the golf ball go straight down the middle of the fairway about 150 yards! He was a natural! But nowadays, I only had time to play once every couple of months or so. The trade-off was well worth it, although a hole in one was still unchecked on my bucket list!

Ben came around the corner and saw me checking out the course. "Did you bring your clubs?" he asked, grinning.

I squinted as I looked back at my son. "Good morning, Ben. No, unfortunately I didn't."

"Too bad because we probably have time to play a round! Although I don't think Heather would appreciate that!" Ben laughed at his own joke. "How are you feeling this morning, Dad?"

I forced a slight grin. "I'll be fine as long as the Tylenol lasts!"

❖ ❖ ❖

Heather arrived a short time later with her mom and dad. She ran quickly into a small room near the entrance of the clubhouse, which had been set up just for the girls. She believed in the tradition of not letting the groom see the bride on her wedding day before the ceremony. It was a tradition that had been around for centuries, although no one was certain of the origin. My wife told Heather that she thought it had started during the times when marriages were arranged; the two people to be wed were never allowed to see each other. Marriages in biblical times were like business deals between two families. A father wanted his daughter to be wed to a man from a rich, land-owning family, which spelled prosperity and fortune for his daughter. But if the groom met the bride before the wedding and wasn't attracted to her, he could back out and cancel the wedding. That was something the family of the bride wanted to avoid, especially if they wanted to secure marrying into a wealthy family. This was also the case for family members who were giving a dowry—they were paying the groom, in effect, to take the daughter as his wife.

While Heather knew Ben wouldn't back out, she did believe it just wouldn't have the same effect if he were to see her before the wedding. So much time and effort would go into her hair, make-up, and the dress that she felt it was a way of keeping the ceremony magical.

My wife and the other bridesmaids filed into the clubhouse, giggling, as they attempted to keep Heather secluded. When Ben and I walked past the door, Hilary, my daughter, came running out and gave us a hug.

"Hi, Dad, sorry I haven't been able to spend much time with you guys. All the girls are pretty busy keeping Heather calm."

"Is she nervous?" I asked, concerned.

"I think she'll be alright, but we're not taking any chances. Well, gotta go!" Hilly turned and smiled at her big brother and added, "Are *you* nervous?"

Ben laughed. "I'm fine. It's Dad you should be worried about."

Hilary turned toward me with a frown. "Still sick, Dad?"

I rubbed my stomach and said, "I'm afraid so. I'll go get checked out right after the wedding. Hey, there's the photographer, you better go." I pointed back to the door where a few bridesmaids were leaning out and yelling for Hilary. The photographer appeared behind them, holding up his camera.

Soon after that, the make-up artist arrived, along with the hair-stylist. Everything was finally underway.

❖ ❖ ❖

As weddings go, it was perfect, and it was everything that Ben and Heather could have hoped for. The weather was beautiful, the country club was absolutely gorgeous, and the food was fabulous. It lasted a little longer than I was hoping for, but I was torn. On one hand, I was hoping for a short ceremony due to the pain in my belly, and on the other hand I wanted it to last forever.

I realized that this was a huge event in my life. My firstborn son was getting married and I couldn't be more proud. Here was my little boy, all grown up and starting a family of his own. I barely held back the tears as I watched Ben and Heather recite their vows.

Soon there would be grandkids, which meant that I would officially be considered old! I would have a hard time calling my-self Grandpa and then wondered if my grandchildren would call me Grandpa or if they would choose something else. When Ben was little, he had started calling my mom Boppin, so it wouldn't be out of character for his kids to find their own names too. No one really knew where that name had come from, but it stuck. She had been Boppin ever since! In fact, my mother had a total of eleven grand-children and each one called her Boppin.

Funny how kids do that, I thought to myself, watching my son.

I was really happy for my son and new daughter-in-law. Immediately after the reception, all of our close family members were going to meet at Heather's parents' house to watch the newly married couple open presents. Their home was large enough to fit everyone who wanted to continue the celebration. It was an expansive tri-level home, built on the side of a mountain, with a beautiful view of Ventura and the Pacific Ocean. After the reception, I helped Ben take the gifts to the car and took him aside.

"Ben, I can't stay. I'm feeling so bad, I've got to get to a hospital and get checked out. I haven't slept in over twenty-four hours and I'm ready to drop! I'm really sorry, I'm afraid something might be seriously wrong."

Ben looked concerned. "Dad, I understand. Thank you for every-thing. We're leaving for our honeymoon in the morning, but we'll only be a couple hours away. I'll call and check up on you tomor-row." Ben was planning on spending two weeks in Palm Springs with Heather. He had booked a beautiful room and had reserved plenty of massage time for the two of them. It was supposed to be a very relaxing getaway, but I knew this little problem of mine was going to be a distraction. I also knew that if I needed Ben, he would come rushing home immediately.

"Please don't worry about me, Ben. I'll be just fine. You have a great honeymoon and I'll see you when you get back. Have a great time. And congratulations!"

Ben looked at me and I could see that he was growing even more concerned. He'd never seen me in this kind of shape. I had always been the kind of father to keep my feelings to myself. I like to portray strength and ability to my kids. I didn't like to show a vulnerable side. They all knew that I was somewhat sensitive, but they also knew that I didn't like to show it. Seeing me giving in to this sickness just proved how bad it was.

"OK, Dad, but just remember, I'm only a phone call away."

While tears formed in his eyes, I hugged my son, patted him on the shoulder, and said goodbye.

CHAPTER 6
MY NEAR-DEATH EXPERIENCE

My son worked in the medical field in Santa Barbara for several years and was familiar with the Ventura hospitals. He suggested I go to Ventura County Medical Center since he felt they had a reputable emergency department and would be able to give me excellent care, whatever the problem was! I was having a difficult time staying awake and walking into a very crowded hospital was not exactly helping matters. I'm not sure what I was expecting at nearly midnight on a Saturday night. The waiting room was packed, which I took as a sign that I would have to wait even longer to solve the mystery of my stomach flu. I knew I had waited too long to seek care, but I hadn't wanted to be a distraction at my son's wedding. I certainly didn't want to take away from our new daughter's special day. And I'm a guy. We never go to the doctor!

I found an open seat and sat down while my wife got me checked in. I rested my head in my hands and drifted in and out of consciousness. All of a sudden, a nurse burst through the double doors and yelled my name. I got up slowly and we made our way to the triage area. The nurse started asking me questions about my symptoms. I told her I thought I had the flu. My wife looked at me and her expression wasn't exactly what I would call pleasant. She told the nurse I had been sick since we arrived in town Wednesday afternoon. My symptoms were pain in the abdomen, a fever, sweating, and I hadn't gone to the bathroom in a couple days.

I looked at the nurse and said, "We're here for our son's wedding. He got married today. I didn't want to be a distraction."

"Congratulations," she said, smiling back. "We will need to get some blood work." She handed me a gown. "Everything off and slip this on, opening in the back."

I changed into the gown and lay down on the examination table. Just then, a guy dressed in scrubs came in and took a few vials of blood. I hate that part of going to the hospital. I'm one of those guys who can't watch them take my blood. For some reason it makes me sick to my stomach. I must have had a bad experience at some point in my past and buried that memory! When the nurse returned, she checked my vitals and found my blood pressure was slightly elevated. She went on to take my temperature and looked closely at the thermometer in surprise.

"Yep, you have a fever alright—104.3!" I looked at my wife, who gave me another stern look. I knew what she was thinking. Yes, I realize I waited too long to get checked out, but I was sure everything would be just fine. The nurse grabbed a small rubber mallet from a table nearby and tapped the bottom of my left foot. "Does this hurt?"

I laughed. "No, of course not!" But when she tapped the bottom of my right foot, the pain in my abdomen made me scream. It was excruciating!

The nurse looked at my wife and said, very businesslike, "It's his appendix. Judging by his fever, the chances are pretty good that it's ruptured already. If it hasn't ruptured, you'll have surgery and go home in a couple days. If it has, you'll be here for four or five days.

But we'll wait for your blood test results to confirm. I'm going to call in a surgeon. The doctor on call tonight is Dr. Kubrick. He's the best."

❖ ❖ ❖

An hour later, Dr. Kubrick walked in and introduced himself. He was a tall man, over six feet, and already wearing his green scrubs. He was soft spoken with grey hair and glasses.

He introduced himself and was looking over my chart and blood test results. "Your white blood cell count is extremely high." He paused and walked around to my side and laid his hands on my belly. "That's a good thing because it means that your body is fighting this infection. But it's also bad because it tells me that your appendix has more than likely ruptured, maybe as long as two or three days ago. Have you been feeling ill for a few days?"

I answered begrudgingly, "Yeah, really sick the past few days. I thought it was just the flu."

"Well, it's not the flu! I'm going to assume that your appendix has ruptured, but I won't know until I get there." He asked, "Have you done any unusual physical activity in the past few days?"

I thought for a couple seconds and answered, "I played home run derby with my boys Wednesday."

The doctor looked at me with a funny look. "Wednesday?" he asked. I nodded. The doctor gently pushed on my abdomen. "Does this hurt?"

"No."

Dr. Kubrick moved his hand around, feeling as he went. "What about this?"

I winced. "A little bit."

"OK. Well, let's get you into surgery and see what's going on in there. I think I should warn you both, if your appendix ruptured Wednesday, we need to get in there right away. I'm going to go in through your belly button first. Since we aren't completely convinced that your appendix has ruptured, it's a good way to start.

I can go in and look around before I decide how to get this thing fixed. Hopefully I can do everything from that first small incision. I would hate to cut up your belly if I don't have to! Let's get you into surgery. I'll see you in a bit."

"Thanks, Doctor. Sorry for calling you in so late."

The doctor smiled. "No problem."

Another nurse came in just after the doctor left and told me that she would be taking me to surgery. I looked at my wife and thought how quickly life could turn. A few hours ago, I had been at my son's wedding, watching one of the most important and memorable days of his life—a day I had tried desperately to enjoy. Now, a couple hours later, I was heading for surgery!

It reminded me of a time when I was a teenager, hunting with my father. My father took me dove hunting every year at the end of summer. It was something I had always looked forward to, especially since the first day of dove season landed on or around my birthday. This particular morning, I had watched a hawk circling in the sky. Suddenly the hawk dropped straight down to Earth to swoop up a field mouse in his claws. It struck me at the time how ironic it was that one minute that poor little mouse was running along, unaware of any looming danger, then the next minute the mouse was gone, reduced to no more than hawk food. That made an impression on me and the memory came rushing back in an instant. A memory I had never forgotten.

That's how life was for some people. One minute, you're happy, enjoying all that life has to offer, like attending your son's wedding. Then the next, it all ends. I hoped that memory would not become a metaphor for my life and that it wouldn't end as abruptly as that little field mouse, but the tone in Dr. Kubrick's voice wasn't too comforting. It might have been just my imagination, but I didn't think that the doctor seemed too positive. Maybe it was the fact that my emergency had called him in at nearly midnight on a Saturday night. Or maybe it was the fact that I had waited too long to seek medical attention. After all, if I had gotten checked out at the first sign of trouble, things would have been better already. But I probably would have missed my son's wedding. Now I was stuck with the circumstance I had created. There was no other path to take other than the one I was on. Besides, it could have just all been my imagination. I could only hope and pray that things would be just fine.

As the nurse wheeled me down the hall and turned a corner, we passed a restroom. I asked the nurse to stop for a moment. She helped me to my feet and I walked into the restroom and closed the door. There I leaned on the sink and looked at myself in the mirror. "You don't look so good, Mike," I said to myself, gazing at my pale skin and the big black circles under my eyes. "You already look dead!"

I sat down on the toilet seat, closed my eyes, and began to pray. *Lord, please be with me during surgery and be with the doctor. Please guide his hands. Help me get through this and heal quickly. Lord, be with my family and give them peace.*

I paused and thought about the last few days and how much fun they were. I loved having a big family and loved spending time with them. I began to tear up suddenly and swallowed hard. I felt very lucky to have lived such a fun, fulfilling life surrounded by a great family. That was what I should be focusing on, not the possibility of it all being over.

Lord, I know I don't thank You enough for all the blessings... but thank You. You've been really good to me. I love you, Lord. In Jesus's name I pray, Amen.

I got up and walked back out to the hall where the nurse was waiting with the gurney. I struggled to climb back up and lie down as every little movement became more and more painful. My wife looked at me as if she was waiting for the details of what had just happened. I just rubbed my belly and smiled, thinking that she didn't need to know about my thoughts and fears. She would have enough of her own at the moment.

The nurse began pushing the gurney again, taking me a little further down the hall. Then she turned to my wife and said, "You two better say goodbye here. There's a waiting room at the end of this hall. The doctor will come find you when he has some news. Until then, make yourself comfortable, it will be at least a few hours."

My wife leaned down and gave me a quick kiss. I smiled at her and whispered, "Everything will be fine, you'll see."

"I'm really worried about you. You're really sick, and I hate to say it, but you don't look so good. I hate that the doctor said he has to get in there to find out what's going on."

I again tried to reassure her. "Honey, they said he's a great doctor, remember? The nurse said he's the best! And Ben said this is the best hospital around! I know I don't look that great, but it's going to be OK, you'll see." I patted her arm. "I'll see you in a couple hours. I love you."

She stood quietly sobbing as the nurse wheeled me and the gurney a few more feet down the hall and threw open the surgery doors. The room was cold and I shivered as the temperature started to sink in. I closed my eyes as two attendants moved me from the gurney to the cold, metal surgical table. The table seemed so small. I had nowhere to put my hands. One of the OR nurses grabbed my hands and folded them on top of my chest. All I could think was, *God, don't let me be the field mouse today!*

❖ ❖ ❖

I looked to my right before any mask was put on to put me to sleep or before any medication was pushed through the IV and saw Jesus standing in the doorway. I thought I must be seeing things, maybe mistaking the surgeon for Jesus. I rubbed my eyes and looked again. This was no surgeon; this was Jesus! He looked into my eyes and held out his hand, gesturing for me to grab ahold. "I want to answer your prayer," He said.

I struggled to make sense of this situation. The last thing I remember before surgery was talking with a doctor about it, being wheeled down the hall on a gurney, and saying goodbye to my wife. "Wait a minute; did I already have the surgery? If not, I should be in surgery right *now*," I said aloud. "Or maybe I should be done by now." I really had no idea what was happening. I felt so confused! I didn't know what to think. Jesus was standing before me waiting for me to take His outstretched hand.

What was happening? Was I dead? If so, then what? Was Jesus here to escort me to Heaven? This didn't make any sense. I looked at Jesus, who stood right in front of me. This was real! He was a physical person standing next to me. This was not a ghost or vision floating around the room. This was physical Jesus holding out His hand.

I wanted to reach out, grab Jesus's hand, and hang on, but something inside me said no. I wasn't sure what would happen if I did that, and I didn't want to make any permanent decisions or mistakes. I thought about my wife and kids. Would they be alright? If I took the hand of Jesus, what then? Was that it? I hadn't had a chance to say goodbye to my kids.

I thought again about all the things I would leave behind. I would never meet my grandchildren. I would never see my dog again, play golf, walk on the beach, or drink coffee or wine! There were so many things I still wanted to do; things I needed to accomplish. What about the bucket list, the hole in one? I suddenly felt sad, lonely, and defeated at the thought that this might be the end. I remembered telling my wife that everything would be alright. Now it looked like I'd been wrong. Then again, I'd always had a strange fascination with near-death experiences, although I wasn't sure if they were even real. But I'd heard that most survivors of near-death experiences said that they floated away, looking down to see their bodies lying below them. I didn't see that or experience anything like that, so maybe that meant that I wasn't *actually* dead.

What then? Jesus was standing before me and that had to mean *something*. This didn't make any sense at all, but this was definitely Jesus!

He looked a little different than I had thought he would. His skin was a little darker, more olive in hue. His hair was light brown and shiny, hanging just past His shoulders. His eyes were a vivid greenish blue and seemed to look right through me. When he looked into my eyes, he looked into my soul. This man knew me. He loved me. It's crazy how all that love just flowed into my being. Of course, I was only comparing this Jesus to pictures I had seen as a kid. But I had seen hundreds of pictures of Jesus and all of them looked similar but very different from the man standing before me.

Something told me that this was the real deal. It might have been just a feeling, but that feeling came from deep within. In my heart, there was no question that this was Jesus.

Whatever hesitation had caused me to pause before taking the hand of my savior suddenly vanished. I reached out to take Jesus by the hand.

As if by magic, when I took hold of His hand, we were instantly transported to the top of a mountain, surrounded by fog. I rubbed my eyes, but the fog made it nearly impossible to see anything. This wasn't just your everyday, run-of-the-mill fog. This was bright white, the brightest white I have ever seen. The fog was a blinding white and did not feel moist at all. I held my hand out in front of me and looked but couldn't see it; the fog was too thick.

I felt the ground beneath my feet and felt warmth on my face, even being surrounded by fog! I looked down and saw grass under my bare toes. The grass was a beautiful, deep green. I curled my toes and felt every blade. My senses were heightened to the point where I could count every blade of grass beneath my feet! It was cool and soothing and I knew in an instant how many blades were touching me.

As my eyes adjusted, suddenly the white in front of me began to pull away, from my right to my left. It was as if someone was pulling a giant curtain off a stage! The first thing I noticed was a basketball-sized light off to my right and a few hundred feet away. It was bright white, just like the fog, but somehow it seemed even brighter and it was shimmering. Then this light began to send out small light beams that looked like fluorescent light bulbs. But these light beams were a little fatter and shorter than the bulbs you buy for the lights in your kitchen. They were about two feet long, smooth and rounded on the ends, and they were shimmering, just like the round light source that was sending them. These light beams were zipping by me and filling the space around us. One of them looked like it was coming straight towards my forehead. I panicked and wondered what I should do. *Do I duck?* I was frozen. So I didn't move and it hit me square in the head, just above my right eye. It went right through me and, as it did, it made a soft, buzzing sound and warmed my entire body right down to my toes.

By now the curtain of white fog was completely gone and I was able to see with a clarity that I can only compare to the best television I'd ever watched! It was the most immersive experience ever! Everything was vibrant and crystal clear. The entire scene seemed so alive!

As my eyes continued to adjust, everything took shape. We were standing on the edge of a mountainside. Just below us were small flowers. It looked like a very large field of flowers that stretched all the way down the side of the mountain. The colors of the flowers were all pastel. There were pinks, purples, yellows and light blues. They reminded me of sweet peas in their shape. I always described them as wispy in nature. They seemed to be waving or moving in a slight wind, but there was no wind. They were definitely moving as if they were dancing. At the bottom of the hill I saw a city, but that curtain of fog had now settled over the city so all I could see were rooftops. There was a very large dome in the center of the city. It appeared to be a huge capital dome. It was gold and very shiny. There were other gold domes, although much smaller, scattered throughout the city. There were also white roofs, most of them pointed, like church steeples. One thing I noticed, though; these steeples did not have crosses on their tops. Although I didn't see any people, something inside me knew that this was a bustling city.

On the other side of the city in the valley was another mountain. On the side of that mountain were trees. Those trees were very tall and straight. They had the shape and look of pine trees with dainty, lacy needles. They were a beautiful dark green and shaped perfectly. The tips of the trees were shimmering in the brilliance of the light as if they had diamonds on the tips, with a pearlescent appearance. Above the trees across the valley was a sky that looked like the most beautiful sunset I had ever witnessed, but there was no sun. Just above the trees the sky was a bright red. Above that was orange, then yellow, purple, and finally a vivid blue. I find it difficult to describe these colors because there are no words to convey the vibrancy or vividness. But I'll try.

If you take a picture of a sunset with your phone and edit the picture by adjusting the saturation all the way to one hundred percent, the focus usually looks a bit blurry. The colors were similar to that but without the blurriness, although even that doesn't do it justice. There were colors I can't even describe. The scenery around me was the most beautiful thing I'd ever seen and my heart yearned to pass it along to my family.

I also struggle to describe the feeling I had while standing there holding the hand of Jesus. To sum it up, I felt love. An overwhelming love. I felt acceptance. I felt comfort. I felt at ease and, most of all, I felt at home. But not just any home. I felt as if I were a kid who had never had a home and had just been adopted by a family and that family had the perfect home. Like a family that longed to have a son for hundreds of years and I was him! I was the son they longed for and I was home. I started thinking to myself, *Where am I?* I was still trying to make sense of it. *Am I dreaming? You can't feel things in your dreams can you?* I wondered. *Do you dream in color? Am I capable of conjuring up colors like these, colors I've never seen before?*

Suddenly the light beams began shooting all the way across the valley, over the tops of the buildings, and lit up the sky. It was breathtaking. In a flash, one of the beams hit the diamond on the tip of one of the trees and it burst into hundreds of tiny light beams. It was like a fireworks explosion of bright white. And those light beams shot all across the sky. Then another light beam hit another tree tip and boom—it exploded too, just like the first. Pretty soon more and more light beams found their way to the tree tips and there were white fireworks everywhere! The white fireworks lit up the sky. It was incredible! The colors of the sky with those bright white explosions everywhere was incredible, more incredible than I could ever describe.

In Revelation 21, John says this about his vision of Heaven: "And he carried me away in the spirit to a mountain great and high, and showed me the Holy City, Jerusalem, coming down out of heaven from God. It shone with the glory of God, and its brilliance was like a jasper, clear as crystal." He goes on to also say, "The city does not need the sun or moon to shine on it, for the glory of God gives it light." Did Jesus take me there? I'm humbled beyond description to think that He may have taken me to the same place He took John.

Believe me when I say I'm struggling to do it justice. My eyes were drawn back to the light source, that basketball-shaped pearlescent light source. Just then, Jesus said, "It is the glory of the Lord." As He said that, I was overcome with emotion and that emotion made me weak in the knees and I was unable to stand. I fell to my knees and when they hit the ground, I was violently jolted back to life. I opened my eyes to see a young doctor standing over me. He was asking me questions. "Do you know your name? Do you know where we are?"

I answered each question in my mind and thought, *Of course I do!* Then the doctor asked me again.

I realized I was only answering the doctor in my head, so I parted my lips to speak. My mouth was dry and my lips were chapped so all I could manage to do was whisper.

"My name is Mike."

He smiled and asked once again, "Do you know where you are?"

I had to think for a second. *I was at my son's wedding—oh, and I had surgery.* "I'm in Ventura," I replied in a hushed tone. My body shivered as I spoke; I was freezing! My vision was blurred as I struggled to look around the room. I didn't recognize anyone. My teeth began to chatter, and I asked quietly, "Where is Dr. Kubrick?"

The doctor looked around, relieved, and said, "Okay, he's back." There were quite a few people in the room, all looking at me. They were all wearing blue scrubs.

I felt strange and out of place, as though something had gone quite wrong. I thought to myself, *Where did Jesus go? What the heck is going on here?*

As the attendants and nurses began to leave, they all looked extremely concerned. One of the young men tapped my leg as he walked out. "Take it easy buddy," he said. Then I saw a nurse putting paddles back on a crash cart in the corner.

It was then that it hit me. I gasped and whispered to myself, "I died!"

CHAPTER 7
PNEUMONIA AND JESUS

Twenty-four hours after surgery, I woke up with a very strange feeling in my chest. I glanced at the clock on the wall: 2:00 a.m. I breathed in and out feeling waves of vapor coat my lungs as I struggled to breathe. My lungs felt like a car radiator that had suddenly been plunged under several feet of water; each little opening held a small amount of air, fighting to enter and escape. As I breathed, my lungs quivered under the fluid that seemed to be building inside my chest. Each rise and fall of my chest only resulted in small choppy gasps, which scared me. I was battling to take even the slightest breath.

I reached for the call button to alert the nurses but was so weak that I could barely move my arms. I managed to push the button and ask the nurse on the other end of the radio for help. Within seconds, a nurse was by my side. I explained that I could barely get a breath of air. She immediately put a stethoscope to my chest. She listened intently for a few seconds then looked me in the eye. I will never forget what she said next.

"Oh honey, you're developing pneumonia. You don't want pneumonia!"

She called for more nurses, who came in immediately. One took my temperature, which was a whopping 104.1. Another nurse came in wheeling an oxygen tank. She strapped a small tube under my nose, leading directly into my nostrils, and turned a knob on top of the tank. Immediately I felt the steady flow of pure oxygen enter my lungs. Still another nurse came in carrying an ice blanket and laid it on top of me, tucking in the sides close to my body.

I hadn't felt this scared since finding out I needed emergency surgery just twenty-four hours earlier. *I'm not getting better, I'm getting worse!* I realized.

I was totally frustrated with the situation and suddenly felt as though I couldn't take it anymore. I began kicking my legs violently and let out a loud scream, followed by another. The nurse leaned over and placed her hands on top of my chest, calmly asking me to stop.

"Michael," she said quietly, "calm down. You're going to be alright. Please settle down!" An impulsive outburst like that was out of character for me and I stopped suddenly, ashamed of myself. That was no way to react to this situation, I knew. I guess I let the frustration of my situation get to me. As I strained my eyes to focus on the nurse she continued speaking.

"Michael, you may have built-up frustrations due to your situation and you may be scared, but I promise that things will get better if you relax."

Exhausted, I closed my eyes, trying to follow her orders.

"That's better," the nurse said while she gently patted my chest. "Just relax. That blanket should help bring down the fever pretty quickly."

Some of the nurses left the room, but another group entered. One of them approached me and handed me a hard, plastic tube on a small stand. It had another, smaller tube extending from the bottom with a mouthpiece on top. There were numbers on the side from one to ten, with ten at the top.

"Michael, I want you to start blowing into this. It's a spirometer. It will help clear your lungs. You have some fluid forming and we need to get rid of it. We need to nip this pneumonia in the bud!"

There was that word again—pneumonia. I knew how weak I was and how serious that illness could be. In my condition, I felt that if I developed pneumonia I would most likely die. Is that why Jesus had shown me Heaven? Was my death inevitable? I had waited a long time to go to the hospital and realized I only had myself to blame for the precarious situation I was in! Would it all come to an end now?

I thought back to the first time I felt like I was getting the flu. It had been right after I played home run derby with the boys in the park. Could that twisting from swinging the bat have put too much stress on my appendix? It was certainly possible, especially if my appendix was already swollen. Maybe it all came down to that one game with my boys. How ironic I thought; the one thing in life that brought so much joy could end up killing me!

I tried to hold the spirometer in front of me, but I was so weak that I couldn't hang on. The nurse propped it up on my chest, put my hands around the base, and placed the mouthpiece between my lips, motioning for me to breathe into it. "Do this ten times an hour," she said.

I tried blowing into the tube and moving the little marble like she had shown me, but I could hardly breathe any air at all into the tube and the marble didn't budge. So I tried again, but it still didn't move. I paused, exhausted, and looked up at the nurse.

"You want to breathe hard enough to hold that little marble right here," she said as she pointed about halfway up to the number 5 on the clear plastic tube. "Keep trying. It will get easier."

As I struggled to move the marble, the last nurse remaining in the room sat down. "I'm going to sit with you for a little bit and make sure you're OK," she told me. Everyone else began filing out of the room, their jobs done.

What happened next boggles the mind. Not just my mind, but any human mind! As the nurses were leaving the room, I felt a presence enter. A holy presence.

When I was a child, my mom told me that when her mother passed away, she was at her home. My grandmother had battled cancer for about six months. It was her wish to be home and not in a hospital during those final days. They brought my grandmother home and made her as comfortable as possible in her own bed. My mom told me that when her mother took her last breath, she was surrounded by her husband, my mom, and a few other family members. My mother told me that she felt a holy presence enter the room just before my grandmother passed away. I asked her for more of a description of what she meant several times, but every time I asked, she welled up with emotion and told me she couldn't describe it any other way. I knew it made her uncomfortable, so I finally stopped asking. I always wondered about that event and what that must have felt like. Now I knew and that memory flooded back. I knew exactly how she felt because I felt it too.

At that moment, Jesus entered the room. I could not see His face this time. But just as it had been twenty-four hours earlier, when the savior of the world enters into your presence, you will know. The Bible says in Romans 14:11, It is written: "'As surely as I live,' says the Lord, 'every knee will bow before me; every tongue will acknowledge God.'" I've always known what that meant, but being in the presence of the Lord will drop you to your knees. Just like during my near-death experience (NDE), when Jesus said to me, "It's the glory of the Lord," I fell to my knees. It wasn't voluntary. I immediately lacked the ability to stand. I believe everyone will eventually know exactly how that feels. Every knee will certainly bow. Every single man, woman, and child. Every believer and unbeliever will bow and acknowledge our maker.

Jesus spoke. "I had to get you away from all the distractions and put you flat on your back so you could hear me."

I was shocked to hear His audible voice, as if He were standing right next to me. I thought His choice of words was interesting. He didn't say, "so you *would* hear me," but he said, "so you *could* hear me." I have to admit, I had been under so much stress the few months leading up to my NDE. I was working as a superintendent for a real estate company. I was in charge of anywhere between thirty to thirty-five homes at various stages of construction. My job was to schedule the work for each house, walk through every home, every day, to make sure contractors showed up on the days they were supposed to, and check to make sure all the work was done by the contractors the previous day. I was also in charge of making sure the job was done correctly, according to the blueprints, that any changes were made that the sales department had told us to make, and to make sure the quality was up to our company standards. Then I had to schedule all the work for my houses and make sure all the contractors were notified. Not to mention putting out any "fires" that came up during the day or, at times, on days I wasn't even on the jobsite. And believe me, when you have over thirty houses under construction, there are always fires! Phew, I'm tired and stressed just writing this!

Okay, I'll stop right here for a moment because I had the same reaction to this that you are having right now. This had to be some sort of hallucination or just my imagination. My fever was still pretty high, I was obviously very sick, and now I was under the influence of medication. But, just like before, this was real.

I looked at the nurse sitting a few feet away. She obviously did not hear the voice of Jesus as He spoke. I looked at her, wanting some sort of acknowledgement. "Did you hear that?" I asked. She looked a bit bewildered and said she didn't hear anything. Then, like the good nurse that she was, she reminded me, "Try to move the marble again." So I breathed into the tube but, just like before, the marble stayed where it was, right on the bottom of the spirometer. I still didn't have enough breath to even get it to roll! But I wasn't going to give up. The presence of Jesus had given me inspiration and the motivation I desperately needed. I wanted to live.

I thought about my family. I thought about actually having grandkids and what that would look like for the first time in my life. I had no idea what the future held for me, but I wanted to be there for it. Yes, I wanted to live even after Jesus had shown me Heaven. It was an overwhelmingly beautiful place. But that was not my home yet. My home was here, with a loving family who were very worried about me. I couldn't give up on them. Not now. Not yet. I pulled the spirometer up to my lips again and breathed. As I did I saw the little marble move. It didn't leave the bottom of the tube, but it moved. Just a little spin, but that was good enough for now. I looked at the clock. It was 2:15 a.m.. I asked Jesus if He was still there. "Yes," I heard him say, "I am right here and I am not going to leave you."

So I looked at the nurse and spoke out loud. "Can you hear me?" I asked.

I expected her to say something back. But she was silent. Then Jesus said, "Yes, Michael, I hear you."

What was happening? The thought of hallucinations entered my mind again. I thought maybe everything had been a hallucination. The trip to Heaven and now this. Could it have been just a figment of my imagination? A few things came to mind. First, I was thinking clearly in the moment, both yesterday and now. I knew to ask the nurse if she could hear me. I never faded in and out of sleep or consciousness. Although my body was weak and my fever was high, I still felt sharp in my mind. *Can you interact with a hallucination?* I wondered. It just didn't add up. I thought back to my experience with Jesus in Heaven. My knees hit the ground at the exact moment that they shocked me back to life. That's amazing timing!

I figured I could ask Jesus. So I did. "Is this real? Are you actually here?" I asked.

I got an answer immediately. "Yes, Michael, this is real. I am here. As I told you before, I need to talk to you without distractions."

Okay, so I got my answer and was ready and anxious to hear what He had to say. But that wouldn't be the last time I asked. Jesus spoke again. "I am pleased with your walk, your faith, and the direction of your path, but I am going to ask more of you. I already know the response you are going to give me, but know this: I am not here to negotiate!" I think at this point my mouth dropped open. *Jesus wants more from me? Who am I? I'm a guy working in the construction industry.*

As they say in the Bible, that was my harvest field! Sure, most of the people I work with can be a little rough around the edges and could use a little "religion," but they're good people. And they already know that I am a Christian. I used to go to church with one of the owners of the company. In fact, that's how I ended up with the job! We attended the same class before church. While I didn't go every week, at least at first, I really grew to love the people in the class. I think it was our way of meeting more as a small group than as a Sunday school class. That was back before small groups were a thing. It seems like every church has small groups now. Most meet outside of church somewhere, either in homes or restaurants. I really like that trend. If you think about how the church got started, back in Jesus's day, it was small groups meeting in homes. I'm getting off on another tangent. If you haven't noticed yet, I'm pretty good at that!

So, one day, my small group leader was late to class and I started talking to Bob, the boss of the company. He told me he was having a tough time filling a superintendent position in his company and asked if I was interested. At first, I wasn't very interested, but I told him I'd consider it. So a few weeks went by and I eventually went in and talked to him and his sister, who was his business partner, and they made me an offer I couldn't refuse! So after a few years, here I was, flat on my back!

"Are you sure this is real?" I asked again.

Jesus chuckled. "Yes, it's real." And, yes, Jesus chuckled. He is the inventor of humor after all.

Once again, the nurse sitting next to my bed did not hear me speak. *Has Jesus muted my voice?* I wondered. There was more proof that this was no hallucination! This was a Holy intervention.

Jesus continued. "I have chosen you to do more for my Kingdom." I have to admit I got a little nervous at that statement. I thought about Moses. The Bible said God spoke to Moses in the form of a burning bush. He also spoke to him face-to-face in a "Tent of Meeting." *Was this my Tent of Meeting?* I thought.

Jesus paused. I'm sure He knew I had to process this. The Bible says that God knows our thoughts, so Jesus gave me a minute. When God told Noah to build the ark, people thought Noah was crazy. He was mocked and shamed. I'm not crazy about that thought. Was I prepared for that? And is the Kingdom of God worth a little shame and harsh words? Absolutely.

I looked around the hospital room for a burning bush or a tent, but there was nothing but sterile white walls and Jesus asking me for more. Maybe that was something special for those courageous men of God. But God doesn't need fanfare when He speaks. This was a simple but very effective meeting with my savior. I was so humbled. I started to weep as Jesus spoke again. "When the time is right, I will give you the words. I will speak to you and you will know what steps to take and what to say. I will open up opportunities for you as well. Remember that everything you are about to go through I have already approved. I will be with you."

I finally spoke back. "Tell me what is going to happen. You know me. You created me. I don't like mysteries!"

I breathed into the spirometer again as Jesus kept speaking. "You will make a full recovery from this and at the right time I am going to send you out into the world to tell our story." I asked what that would look like. Was I supposed to write a book? Was I going to be a speaker or evangelist? That would be a giant step for me!

Jesus continued, "But first, you will have some trials and changes. You have some valleys to walk through. It is necessary. Remember, I will be with you and giving you courage."

I realized He said courage a couple times and, to be honest, it was a little frightening. Courage is needed in times of fear or uncertainty. God has always helped me overcome fear. When I was a kid, I was deathly afraid of the dark. I was also afraid of monsters under my bed. At times, that fear actually kept me frozen under my covers, afraid to move. But as I grew up, the Lord revealed the untruth of my childhood fears. I realized that everything is the same in the dark as it is in the light. The only thing different is the light! Some might say that's just part of growing up. And maybe they're right. But as a kid just beginning a walk in Christianity, I choose to believe that God guided my steps.

I asked Jesus to be more specific, but I didn't get an answer. So I asked again. A few minutes later, He told me that details are not important. He told me to remember that He would be with me and guide me. He told me to trust Him. That's hard to do sometimes, especially during trials. It sounded like He was preparing me for something big. And I found out a few years later just how big it would be.

Just then, the nurse stood up and took my temperature. "Good news," she said. "You're down to 100.5. I'm going to leave the ice blanket on a little longer. How's your pain?"

"I'm fine," I said.

I found it difficult to talk to her while Jesus was still in the room. It was so bizarre! But something occurred to me while she was standing over me, listening to my lungs with her stethoscope. My temperature was slightly over one hundred. That wasn't high enough to produce a hallucination. So there was the proof I needed. I was not hallucinating. I wasn't under the influence of pain medication that might cause crazy dreams. Jesus was, in fact, here in the room with me. I was truly experiencing something Holy. This was real. I smiled at the thought, and I could sense Jesus was pleased.

He spoke again. "Michael, breathe again." I blew into the spirometer and the little ball moved up in the tube to number two! I was ecstatic! I did it! I was on my way to beating this setback. Jesus said, "I will let you know what direction I want you to take soon. Stay open to hearing my voice. I'm going to use this experience to reach millions."

What? I was blown away and found that a little hard to believe! Millions? *Who am I to speak to millions? That's Billy Graham territory! I'm just a regular guy working in the construction field.* But the thoughts of Moses and Noah flooded back into my mind. Was it actually possible? I thought. *Yes, of course it is. With God, anything is possible. But I've never been someone who is comfortable talking to large crowds. Heck, I don't like talking to small crowds. But Jesus did say He would tell me when the time was right.* I figured God needed to work on me. I didn't know at that point what witnessing to millions could even look like. I'm not a writer, but did God want me to write a book? That thought entered my mind again. *Did God plant that thought?* I wondered. Maybe. But I had to trust Him.

"Is there anything else I need to know, Lord?" I asked.

"Michael, you need to know that when you step out in faith, the enemy steps up his attacks."

Yikes, I thought. *I don't like attacks.* A Bible verse came to mind in that moment. Store up your treasures in Heaven. I'm paraphrasing. The quote is from the book of Matthew 6:19–21. "Do not store up for yourselves treasures on earth, where moths and vermin destroy, and where thieves break in and steal. But store up for yourselves treasures in heaven, where moths and vermin do not destroy, and where thieves do not break in and steal. For where your treasure is, there your heart will be also." That was what Jesus was telling me. No matter how much trouble I would face in the future, it would be worth it because I would be doing this for the Kingdom. I would literally be storing up treasures in Heaven!

Then Jesus spoke to me for the last time and it was really cool. He said, "Let's stay in touch."

"Don't worry. I will talk to you more than ever. Thank you for answering my prayers, Lord. I'm all in! But please don't leave. Not yet. I have so many more questions."

Being the gentleman that He is, Jesus agreed. "Michael, I can answer your questions, but you must understand that you have an earthly perspective. You do not have the capability to fully comprehend the future. I have told you I will be with you. I will guide you and provide you comfort. You are already under the protection of angels."

"Wow," I said. My mouth must have hung open for a while. Jesus just told me I have guardian angels. *This is getting serious*, I thought.

Jesus continued, "You have been set apart and called for a purpose. Just follow my lead and you will be fine. You will have some heartaches and some valleys to walk through. You will feel pain. But you will feel my love as well. Remember, I have approved all of that. So just keep talking to me and keep walking through them."

When he said, "them," I knew that meant more than one. I got a little frightened. No one likes heartache. I certainly didn't want to walk through a valley. I thought of the valley of the shadow of death mentioned in the Bible. I felt like I was already there. So I asked, "Heartaches and valleys?"

I think Jesus was getting tired of my persistence. He simply said, "Yes. Trust me."

I nodded and said, "I trust you."

Over the next hour or so, I managed to get the little ball in the spirometer moving and used it so often that night that my lungs had cleared in three hours. I was awake until about 5:00 a.m.. After the talk with Jesus and all that breathing, I was exhausted. The last thing I remember about that long night was the nurse listening to my lungs and saying, "I think you beat it, Mike." I was overjoyed.

I felt such a sense of accomplishment. I was hoping to live. But Jesus had already told me that. I guess, in the moment, I lacked a little faith. Now I had to concentrate on getting healthy and waiting on the Lord to give me my marching orders!

Early the next morning, a nurse came in and took my temperature. It was under one hundred for the first time since I checked in. But it had still spiked at night to just over one hundred. I wasn't quite ready to go home. *Be patient*, I thought. *God will use everything as a testimony.* He had said I would reach millions. I had to have confidence that whatever this time in the hospital was going to accomplish, it would bring glory to His Kingdom.

The next day, when my wife came to visit me, the first thing I said was, "You've got to bring me a notebook and a pencil or pen. I have to start writing things down."

She looked surprised but said, "I'll run out and get you something in the gift shop." She turned and left rather quickly. I didn't mean she had to get something that instant, but it was necessary. I had to document everything Jesus had told me. And I had to write down every single detail of the visit to Heaven that Jesus had taken me on. If I was going to write a book, I had to document the details. *I can't misrepresent Jesus!* I thought.

CHAPTER 8
NOT OUT OF THE WOODS YET

Day by day I got stronger, but the persistent fever remained. Dr. Kubrick ordered scans every day, trying desperately to find the source of the elusive infection. Apparently he suspected I had developed an abscess and, if I had, it should show up on a scan of my abdomen. I hated the process of going downstairs for a scan, though I realized that it was necessary. I'd already gone through the process three times and now I was scheduled for another one.

An hour before the scan, I had to drink a quart of the most disgusting flavored chalky milk I had ever tasted. The concoction smelled like a mixture of rotten fruit and stinky feet. The aftertaste was even worse, with hints of copper and ammonia. Each time, I chugged a mouthful of the quart then stopped to catch my breath. It took at least half an hour to finish off the remainder.

Doctor Kubrick remained convinced that I must have an abscess somewhere, although it hadn't shown up on any of the previous scans. The fact that they were unable to find it was frustrating to me.

After my morning walk, pushing my IV stand up and down the halls, I climbed back into bed and lay down, exhausted. Walking was helping build my strength, but it still tired me out. I looked at the tray next to my bed and there, amongst my box of Kleenex, magazines, and phone, was the empty jar from that morning's preparatory scan juice. The chalky substance left a streaky white film on the walls of the container. I could smell it, even from a few feet away. *That stuff is disgusting,* I thought. The unpleasant aroma brought back all the frustration of numerous scans leading to negative results. Day by day, my frustration mounted and it was taking its toll on my daily outlook. I was sinking lower and lower every day.

Finally, one of my nurses walked in and told me the news I'd been waiting for since waking up after surgery. "Well, Michael, your latest scan came back negative again, so your doctor is going to let you resume a normal diet!"

"But what about the fever?" I asked.

"Nothing is showing up on your scans or blood tests, so he's probably decided that it's a very slight infection. I'm sure he's convinced that antibiotics will kill the remainder of the E. coli. It won't get any worse if you eat solid food. I've ordered your dinner. It should be here in a few minutes."

The thought of real food was very exciting to me. I had been on a strict liquid diet since surgery and had already lost almost twenty pounds in the week I'd been there. Lately, when I finished a liquid meal of beef broth, I was still hungry. I couldn't wait to eat "real food" again, hospital food or not! My dinner was brought in as my nurse left my room.

The orderly placed the tray down and raised my bed to a sitting position. I couldn't believe my eyes as the young woman lifted the top of the tray. Meatloaf, mashed potatoes and gravy, a fresh banana, some pudding, and milk. I never thought such a bland meal could look so delicious!

I grabbed the banana and started peeling. As I took my first bite, I began to weep. Here I was in a hospital, having barely survived a brush with death, and now this banana—something grown hundreds of miles away, out of the dirt of the earth—was helping make me healthy. I was blown away by the simplicity, and complexity, of it all. It was all such a miracle. The thought of God's creation hit me like a ton of bricks.

I laid my head back on my pillow and closed my eyes, remembering a conversation I'd had with a friend not long ago. This particular friend was not a believer in God and I remembered asking him how it was possible to look at everything God had created and still not believe in a creator. Like most people who don't believe, he just shrugged it off as a fairytale. The earth somehow just created itself through a "Big Bang." That never made sense to me. It had to start with something! Personally, I think it takes more faith to believe in creating something out of nothing, and creating life from non-life, than it does to believe in God. *How could anyone live on this earth and witness the sustainability of life and not believe in God?* I wondered.

The aroma of the meatloaf wafting just below my nostrils brought me back to reality and made my taste buds salivate. I open-ed my eyes and continued my meal, quickly piercing a hunk of meatloaf, swirling the loaded fork through the mashed potatoes and gravy, and stuffing it into my mouth. I moaned as I chewed. *Oh, so good,* I thought. I took a few more bites of meatloaf and closed my eyes again, savoring every morsel.

Just then a nurse ran into the room and yelled, "Stop eating!"

"Huh?" I asked, my mouth still full of meatloaf and mashed potatoes.

"They found an abscess!"

I spit my mouthful of food out onto the tray, deflated. After a week and four scans they had finally found the cause of the infection. And right in the middle of my first meal.

"How much did you eat?" asked the nurse.

"I ate the banana, a couple bites of the meatloaf, and some potatoes, not counting the bite I just spit out!"

"Don't eat anymore. I'll be right back."

I fell back on the bed, disappointed. That was the last thing I had expected to happen and the timing couldn't have been worse! Still, I supposed I should count my blessings—if eating was going to make the abscess worse, it was better that the nurse had caught me before I ate too much. The last thing I needed was for the infection to cause another setback.

The nurse came back a few minutes later. "Ok, I just spoke with the doctor. You're going to go NPO at midnight and then tomorrow morning they're going to go in and get the abscess, so you can finish your dinner."

"NPO?" I asked. "What's that?"

She smiled and said, "It's a Latin term; it means nothing by mouth!" I nodded and she waited for my response. "Aren't you happy? You're one giant step closer to being able to go home and you get to finish your dinner!"

"I guess," I said. I nibbled on the remaining meatloaf. "Are you sure it's okay to finish?"

The nurse smiled and looked at me empathetically. "Sure."

❖ ❖ ❖

"Mike McKinsey?"

"Yeah." I recognized the young man in the white coat standing in front of the empty wheelchair. It was the transporter from X-ray, waiting to take me for my latest procedure.

"So what all is involved in getting an abscess?" I asked as I walked toward the wheelchair.

The transporter laughed. "Oh, it's fun, Mike, you're going to love it!"

"Why do I detect a rather large amount of sarcasm?" I asked as I sat down in the wheelchair, grimacing; movement was still somewhat difficult for me.

As the transporter covered my legs with a blanket, he smiled and said, "You'll see, Mr. McKinsey. It can't be *that* bad, although I don't remember anyone I've transported having this done!"

"Oh, that's just perfect!"

The two of us laughed as we began the long descent down the hall, then three floors down to the X-ray department.

I was wheeled into the scan room, where a nurse greeted me. She told me to lie down on my stomach this time, on a long, cold stainless steel bed, covered only by a thin sheet of white paper. Every other scan I had done while lying on my back and I asked about the change.

The nurse began to explain the procedure. "Well, Mike, here's the deal. The abscess is at the very bottom of your abdominal cavity. We can't go in through the front because you have too many organs in the way. We need a straight shot to the abscess, so we're going in through your backside."

"What do you mean by 'your backside'?" I asked, already a little scared.

"What I mean is, um, we go through your butt cheek."

"What?" I raised my head and looked at her. "Are you serious?"

"It gives us a clear path directly to the abscess."

Just then, a very tall, slender, dark-haired woman walked in. "Hi. Michael McKinsey?"

"Yes."

"I'm Dr. Miller. I'll be performing your procedure today." Dr. Miller looked like she could double as a model. She had a dark complexion and long brown hair, straight and smooth as silk. She was a very striking woman, and she seemed to be at least six feet tall, although from my vantage point it was hard to tell.

I smiled and tried to hide my discomfort. So far this procedure didn't sound like much fun, but it was my ticket out of the hospital.

I had adopted the attitude of go along to get along. Don't fight it, just go along. It will be over soon.

Dr. Miller continued. "Here's the plan. We're going to insert a needle through your gluteus muscle, right here." She took a pen and drew a small dot on my left butt cheek. "Once we penetrate the skin, we will slide you into the tube and take a picture. We'll probably have to do this several times to make sure we're on target to hit the abscess. Once we're in, we will penetrate the abscess, drain it, and leave a drain in for about twenty-four hours. After that, I think you should be clear of all infections and you can go home."

"That's the best news I've heard all week," I said. I felt somewhat relieved, but some of the procedure Dr. Miller just described still made me nervous. What did she mean when she said they'd have to repeat this several times and what did she mean by leaving the drain in? What drain? *Oh well,* I thought, *just go along!*

The doctor and nurse talked for a few more minutes as the nurse disconnected my IV bag. She then connected my IV tube to a new bag, which hovered just above my head, hopefully filled with something to ease the pain I was about to endure.

The nurse grabbed a small valve on the IV bag and gave it a slight twist. "Now, Mike, this will keep you from feeling some pain, but I can't let you have too much at first. Let me know if things get unbearable and I can give you a little more. But I can't give you as much as you'll want; protocol on this type of procedure says that you have to remain conscious, so you're going to feel some of it."

As Dr. Miller left the room the nurse said, "The first thing I'm going to ask you to do is roll over onto your side." I slowly rolled over, and she said, "My name is Janet. If things get unbearable, you call my name and let me know."

Now lying on my side with my legs straight and arms slightly bent in front of me, I said, "Janet, that's the second time you've told me I'm going to be uncomfortable. Is that nurse code for 'this is going to hurt'?"

Janet sat down on a small stool, wheeled it over next to my face, and smiled. "I'm not going to lie to you Mike, this procedure is no fun."

"Thanks for the honesty," I said somberly.

Janet wheeled back around to my backside and said, "Now, the first thing we have to do is fill your rectum with water so it will show up better on the scan. We don't want to puncture anything on the way in." As she said this she inserted a small metal tube into my rectum.

I was shocked. "You're kidding, right?"

"The water is warm, so it won't be too bad," she said with a hint of sarcasm in her voice.

I knew she was doing her best to comfort me. "You really think the fact that it's warm makes it better?" I tried to keep a sense of humor about what was happening back there but was finding it more and more difficult. I said to Janet, "I feel like I'm being violated by R2-D2!" She tried to hide her laughter from me! I was not looking forward to this and it was already well underway.

As Janet started the flow of water, I realized that the water *was* warm, but it was going to get worse. I told myself to just go along and that it would be over soon.

"Doing OK, Mike?" Janet asked.

"So far so good." I was feeling relaxed; *the drugs must be starting to take effect*, I thought.

Dr. Miller came back in the room then, holding a very large needle, the size of a pencil.

I panicked, despite the relaxing medication. "That's going in my ass?" I gasped.

Janet couldn't help but laugh, which drew a harsh look from the doctor. "This is what we use to drain that nasty abscess, Mike. We'll keep you as drugged up as we can, right Janet? And we'll be done before you know it. Hang in there!"

Dr. Miller positioned the needle over the dot she had drawn on my rear end and began to push it into my skin. I let out a scream as the pain hit me.

"Oh, my gosh; that hurts!"

"We have a long way to go, Mike. Be tough."

I looked at Janet and asked if she could give me more pain medication. "I won't make it if it hurts this much," I pleaded.

Janet reached up and adjusted the drip. "That should help."

I could feel the relief instantly, although the pain was still intense. Dr. Miller walked out of the room as Janet held the needle, now protruding out of my butt cheek. She gently let it go, which hurt even more as it now dangled by its own weight.

"A quick trip into the tube for a picture," she said. "Don't move, Mike, I'll be right back."

After Janet slid me and the dangling needle into the tube, she ran around the corner, pushed a few buttons, and powered up the machine. I heard the familiar sound of the scanner snapping pictures and then Janet came running back into the room, slid me back out of the tube, and grabbed the needle. A few seconds later, Dr. Miller came back in and took the needle, still protruding from my butt cheek, from Janet.

"We're right on target," she said. She pushed the needle in a little further. "Time for another picture!"

I groaned again in pain. "Can I get another hit of that stuff?" I motioned up at the IV bag hanging above my head.

"A little bit more should be alright, but we're near the limit, Mike." Janet adjusted the drip again. It had the same effect, immediately easing the pain, and I sighed in relief. She slid me back into the tube, letting go of the needle.

"Be right back," she said as she quickly ran around the corner. Again I heard the familiar buzzing of the machine taking its picture. And just like before, Janet and Dr. Miller came back into the room.

This routine was repeated until Dr. Miller finally said, "Okay Mike, we're in. I'm going to drain it now and get you back up to your room." She slowly pulled the plunger on the needle, draining the abscess. Then she attached a bag to the end of the plastic hose that had replaced the needle protruding from my derrière.

All those doses of medication finally took full effect and the next thing I remembered was waking up in my hospital bed, the entire procedure now seeming like a bad dream. But when I reached around and felt the hose and drain bag, I remembered. That was no dream!

CHAPTER 9
THE HONEYMOONERS RETURN

Ben and Heather decided to come home early from their honeymoon. They had been staying in the honeymoon suite at the Marriott in Desert Hot Springs. Ben had spared no expense when it came to pampering his new bride. Their room overlooked a lake and included a poolside cabana. They had spent ten days in total luxury. But the thought of his father lying in a hospital room was too much for my son. It didn't take much convincing when he asked Heather if she would mind going home a few days early.

When they first left for Desert Hot Springs, I had been through surgery and my wife had let them both know that I would be fine. She didn't tell them all the details of how close it had been. When Ben and Heather got to the hospital eleven days after their wedding and the surgery, it was a shock. Ben gasped when he saw me. I had lost so much weight; it was too much for him to handle and he started to cry.

"Dad, I'm so sorry I wasn't here for you. You look like death warmed over."

I thought back to the past week—my experience with Jesus, going to Heaven, and finally telling my wife after failing so many times. Then there was the whole abscess episode, which was a story all its own. The emotion of the entire ordeal and the sight of my son's tears started to get the best of me.

"There's so much I need to tell you, Ben. But I wish you had stayed on your honeymoon for the full two weeks. There was no reason to come home early; the worst is behind me now."

I looked at my son, who was turning white at my depleted state, and held out my hands. Ben strode over and laid his head in my lap.

"I'm so glad you're going to be alright. You must have been through a lot," he mumbled through the tears.

"You have no idea, Ben; this was rough. It was a pretty close call. Much closer than I care to admit."

"You still have a tube hanging out of you there, Dad." Ben grabbed it loosely and asked, "What's it for?"

"They had to drain an abscess and that's to catch the leftovers!"

"Nice!" Just as Ben said that, Dr. Miller came in. "Hello everyone, hello Mike," she said, looking around the room.

"Hi, Doc," I answered. "Nice to see you again under better circumstances."

"I'm here to remove the drain. Dr. Kubrick says you'll probably be going home tomorrow. Once my tube is out, if your temperature stays normal, you should be good to go."

Ben, Heather, and my wife excused themselves as Dr. Miller pulled the curtain around to shield my bed from the rest of the room. As soon as she did, she went to work. In just a few minutes, the tube was out and I had nothing more than a small bandage covering the incision.

"Sure comes out easier than it goes in, doesn't it, Doc?"

"Sure does, Mike." Dr. Miller laughed. She wished me good luck and left.

When my family saw the doctor leave, they let themselves back in. When they pulled the curtain back, we all noticed that my roommate, Terry, was packing his bags and getting ready to leave. Terry had been my roommate for six days. He was a big guy from New York who had been admitted a week before to undergo colon cancer treatment. Terry had me laughing from the moment I met him. As you may know, laughing and abdomen surgery are not exactly compatible, but he made the hospital stay a little more bearable.

I had woken up one morning to find a new guy in the bed next to me. From the first moment he noticed that I was awake he started talking. He had one of those personalities that filled any space he inhabited and was definitely what you would call "a talker"!

"What are you in for?" he asked on his first morning.

"Ruptured appendix." I turned my head in the direction of the voice, but I was still unable to lift it off the pillow. "But I flatlined a few days ago and I've been under observation since then. I'm happy to get out of the ICU alive. Guess Heaven's not quite ready for me!"

"Wow." The tone of the mysterious voice suddenly changed from funny to anxious.

I looked up towards the ceiling and noticed a handle on the end of a chain a few feet from my head. I had noticed it before, but only now realized why it was there. *It must be so I can pull myself up off the bed; they think of everything*, I thought. I reached up and grabbed the handle, then pulled with all my strength and lifted myself a few inches to turn and look at my new neighbor.

"I'm Mike, nice to meet you." I dropped back down onto the bed, exhausted from the small amount of movement. Lifting my body up had allowed some air circulation between me and the mattress, though, which cooled me. I made a mental note to try it again a little bit later.

"I'm Terry, nice to meet you too." Terry looked like he was about my age. He was a handsome man in his late fifties, slightly overweight, with jet-black hair. "So how's recovery treating you?" he asked. "Going home soon?"

"I certainly hope so, but I've got to get my temperature back down to normal, and I need to get some strength back. This thing almost got me. I already had a couple close calls. And I had this weird dream. I guess you could say I had a near-death experience."

"No shit!" Terry sat up in his bed.

I was surprised at that response and didn't know what to say.

"You've got to tell me about it, man!" my roommate urged.

I thought about the NDE, about Jesus holding my hand, and how we had flown to that mountaintop in the blink of an eye. I thought about all the colors, those spectacular colors. I thought about Jesus's words the next day, how He spoke for hours without the nurse hearing a word. Everything was so awesome, but how could I ever describe it and do it justice? I opened my mouth to tell Terry, but started crying again. I was so humbled by the experience that I was unable to speak. I tried again to tell Terry about my experience, but when I opened my mouth to speak, all that came out were sobs. All I could manage to say was, "Sorry."

What was it about that dream that makes it impossible to tell anyone? I wondered. I should be able to shout that experience from the mountaintops. There is so much to tell. So much of my experience could bring so much hope. It would be so good for everyone who hears it, if I could only tell people. I'm sure that's what Jesus meant when He told me He was going to use me. I should at least be able to tell Terry; I just met him, for goodness' sake!

I realized that I had to get past the sobbing part and find the words to describe the entire experience. It was so magnificent, so wonderful, and I wanted to tell everyone! But I realized I needed to follow the instructions that Jesus had given me a few days earlier. He would tell me when to speak. Maybe now was just too soon.

Terry seemed sympathetic, though, and understood my difficulty in speaking. "Hey, it's ok, I understand. It must have been really something to affect you in that way."

I tried to respond, but once again all I could manage to say was, "Yeah, it was." I closed my eyes and dozed off, hoping and praying to have the same dream again.

I woke up several hours later to Terry trying desperately to get a nurse's attention. "Hello. Hello, anybody there?" he shouted into the intercom system that was supposed to ring directly to the nurses' station. "Is this thing working? Hello!" His voice became panicked with the long silence.

Finally a small voice on the other end answered. "Yes, what can I do for you?" It was a night nurse, answering Terry's page. She spoke in a very heavy accent. "Can I help you, sir?"

Terry answered, "Yeah, hey… I got a little problem here."

"Yes, go ahead. What can I do for you?"

"Well…" Terry paused, embarrassed, and I squeezed my eyes shut. "I either just passed gas… or I crapped my pants." Terry let go of the intercom button and giggled, then spoke softly to himself. "I don't know how to say this delicately."

The tiny voice on the other end said, "Excuse me?"

Terry giggled again and pushed the call button. "I just passed gas or I crapped my pants. I'm really sorry."

The voice on the other end could not understand and asked one more time, "Excuse me, sir, what is it you need?"

Terry, sounding desperate now, said in a loud voice, "I just farted or I *shit my pants*!"

After a long pause the nurse said, "I'll be right there."

I was now completely awake and started laughing after hearing that exchange. When Terry heard me laughing, he started laughing as well.

"Ouch," I finally said. "Stop, it hurts to laugh!"

This made Terry laugh even harder.

A few seconds later, a nurse walked in and saw Terry smiling. "So what happened?" she asked.

Once again, Terry told her his dilemma. "I think I may have crapped my pants! I woke up coughing and, well, it was an accident."

"Well," said the nurse, "let's take a look."

Terry voluntarily rolled onto his side. The nurse leaned over and checked his backside. "Nope, everything is fine!"

Terry sighed. "That's a relief!"

I couldn't help but chuckle at Terry's circumstance, although even the slightest movement in my stomach still hurt.

❖ ❖ ❖

I was sad to see Terry packing up, but I was happy he had recovered so quickly and was given the okay to leave.

"Good luck to you, my friend. I'm going to miss you. What's the prognosis?"

Terry shook his head. "You know, I'm just going to take things one day at a time. Doc says I should be fine, but I think he's going to have me go through some chemo."

"I'll keep you in my prayers, Terry. Thanks for making my stay here so much fun!"

Terry said, "Yeah, there are a few stories I'll never forget, Mike. You take care."

A transporter knocked on the door and Terry sat down in his wheelchair. He saluted me and said, "Later dude!"

After Terry was gone, Ben said, "What a cool guy!"

"Yeah, he was great," I said. "So funny. That guy had me cracking up, even when it hurt to laugh!"

"So Dad, you want to take a quick walk up and down the hall before we get out of here?" Ben asked suddenly.

I smiled, thinking that since my son was in the medical field, he knew how important it was to walk. "You sound like you've been talking to my nurses," I said. "That's a good idea, Ben."

I got out of bed more easily without all of the cumbersome tubes—this was the first time I'd been without them in eleven days. A few days ago, I had joked that I had tubes hanging out of me from places I didn't know they could put tubes in! Once I was out of bed I stretched, happy to have my body almost back to normal. We walked down the hall, past the nurses' station. I stopped and looked out the fourth-floor window toward the ocean.

"I spent lots of time right here," I told them.

"Because of the view?" Ben asked.

"No, because this is the warmest spot in the hall!" I laughed. "In a strange way, I'm going to miss this place." I led the small processional slowly back to my room. Just before I got back in bed Ben asked, "Dad, before I leave, can we pray?"

"I'd love that, buddy," I said softly.

Ben grabbed my hand, along with my wife and Heather. We formed a small circle in the hospital room and Ben led the prayer. "Father, thank you for watching out for my dad while I was away. Thank you for protecting him and giving him a new chance at life. We love You, Lord. Keep him safe and get him out of here tomorrow. Amen."

Ben opened his eyes and looked at the floor below me. Suddenly he screamed. "Dad, you're bleeding!"

I looked down and saw a small pool of blood below me. Before I could react, Ben grabbed me and pushed me onto the bed. He turned me over and saw that the blood was coming from the incision in my butt cheek where the drain had been.

"Call a nurse," Ben shouted at his bride.

Heather grabbed the call button and frantically asked for help. Ben forced me over onto my stomach and pressed his hand over the wound, applying pressure to stop the bleeding. While they waited for a nurse to arrive, Ben tried to relieve the obvious tension in the room. He chuckled and said, "You've got a nice ass, Dad!"

I just muttered, my face buried in the pillows. The girls just laughed.

A few seconds later, a nurse arrived to relieve Ben. A few minutes more and Dr. Miller walked in. She relieved the nurse and looked at the wound, which had already stopped bleeding. As she taped on a new, larger bandage, she said, "That should do it, Mike. You should probably stay in bed the rest of the night to keep the wound from opening up again. No more walking around until tomorrow!"

❖ ❖ ❖

After four days in ICU and another eight days in a general population hospital bed, twelve very long days total, I finally got the approval to be released from the hospital. Since my temperature was back to normal, and had been steady all night, Dr. Kubrick gave me the okay. I'd spent too long in the hospital, but now it was time to get home and return to a normal life; at least as normal as one can have after a near-death experience.

I made some promises to God before I left the hospital. For one, I was going to be sure to tell all my friends and family how much I loved them. I had realized how quickly this precious gift of life can be taken from me and I didn't want to end up being the mouse in the hawk's claws, leaving this earth suddenly without everyone knowing how I truly felt about them. That would have a lasting impact on my entire family and, as far as I could tell, a lasting impact on God's Kingdom.

The other promise I made to God was to become the kind of man I knew He wanted me to be. Not that I had been a bad person, but I knew I needed to be a better person and a better Christian. My wife reminded me all the time to be an "effective witness." At times I felt that I'd become somewhat of a hypocrite. And the one thing I hated was a hypocrite. I always figured they existed because the devil had found a way to become so effective in this lost world.

I was determined to go away from this experience with a renewed sense of what Jesus wanted from true believers. As I saw it, this was a fresh start. And now, with God's help, I had a story—a real story! All I had to do was be patient and listen for God's voice. I started praying every day that He would let me know what to do and when to do it. I vowed to use this new revelation in a brand-new way. I couldn't wait to get home and begin my "new" life.

CHAPTER 10
ANSWERED PRAYERS

God has answered so many prayers in my life that I must share some of them with you. I'm going to tell you about some of the most impactful and dramatic ones, but there are many more that some would call "insignificant." But I believe God uses every answer to prayer in everyone's life to help and guide us to become more of the person He wants us to be. And that's not insignificant. He even uses the prayers that He answers as "no," to mold and shape our lives. Sometimes the hardest thing we can do is realize that only God has the perspective to see how all our prayers affect His children and His Kingdom as a whole. That's tough, but we must always have faith. God knows what is best.

❖ ❖ ❖

My wife and I, along with our son, Chris, were waiting in the lobby of UC San Francisco. We were there to see Dr. Marconi, who was a specialist in movement disorders. I hadn't been to San

Francisco in over ten years and didn't like coming back to the city under the circumstances that were still unfolding.

Chris had been having cramps for two years. He said that he first noticed them when he was playing baseball. When they first started, they were nothing more than slight cramps in his hand or foot. I gave him extra bananas before practice and every game, hoping it was a simple mineral deficiency. Unfortunately, that hadn't helped.

Then, as his sophomore season progressed, things got more intense. The cramps lasted longer and became more debilitating. They hadn't stopped him from playing the game he loved; Chris was brought up to the Varsity squad as a sophomore. It was quite an honor for him, but one he deserved. He dealt with the pain that the cramping brought and managed to get through the season with few people noticing he was suffering. After the season ended, so did the cramps.

But as the next season began, the cramping came back. This time, when Chris ran, he felt tingling in his feet, usually on the left side. The tingling continued up his arm and into his hand. Then his hand would cramp up into a fist, causing enough pain to make him stop whatever he was doing and grab his hand to try to pry it open. Just like the previous year, the cramps only lasted about thirty seconds—just long and severe enough to hinder his game.

More importantly, though, it worried my wife and me to the point that we were afraid something more sinister was going on in Chris's body. We hadn't been able to cure the cramping with bananas, Gatorade, or extra water, so it was far beyond my personal knowledge.

I took my son to the family physician. She prescribed medication, mostly to calm his nerves. Chris tried that for a couple weeks but found that it didn't help with the cramping. We went back to the doctor and she increased the dose, which ultimately had the same outcome; no help at all.

On our third visit, she decided to send Chris to a chiropractor, thinking he may have a pinched nerve somewhere. After a few more weeks with that new doctor, the cramps returned. Now they were affecting his playing time, which was devastating to both Chris and the team.

One doctor led to another doctor, with little help and no progress. This went on for almost two years. While I was exploring the internet seeking a magical cure one night, I came across something so outrageous I thought it might just be the magic bullet we had been seeking. So the night before his next game, I made Chris drink some apple cider vinegar! I had stumbled across a thread that said a kid had been having cramps that sounded like the same type that Chris had been having, and I thought it was worth a shot. Chris never let me live that one down; drinking vinegar was disgusting and, more importantly, it didn't work.

In fact, nothing did. No doctor had an answer. Each doctor sent Chris on his way to a more specialized doctor, telling him that they were baffled. So here we were, in Dr. Marconi's office. It would be the last stop. She was one of the top doctors in the country, specializing in movement disorders, and represented one of our last choices. We'd put her off because her practice was out of our insurance network and because of the distance we would have to travel. Still, we weren't willing to give up without a fight. I had spent all night praying that she'd be able to give us an answer, even if it was one we didn't want to hear.

Dr. Marconi came into the waiting area then and introduced herself. She asked us all to come back to her office and sit down. First she explained about movement disorders. She talked about dystonia, a condition brought on by many different triggers. It was a nerve disorder. I remembered seeing a few videos on dystonia and recalled that all of them had been very scary. Most showed a patient sitting in a padded room and repeatedly jerking into a shriveled-up ball. I begged God that Chris would not have that; I didn't think I'd be able to watch my son turn from a star athlete into a sick young man. The doctor did a quick examination of Chris, then had him try to bring on a cramping episode. She had him run up and down the hall, but he was never able to duplicate the symptoms.

After that, the doctor asked us to come back into the office and sit down. After a little more explaining and investigation of the charts and records, she finally said, "Chris, there's an old joke that goes like this. A man goes to his doctor and says, 'Doc, it hurts when I do this.' The doctor looks at him and says, 'Well, don't do that!'"

She threw his chart on her desk and sighed. "So, unfortunately, that is my advice to you. I can't give you a certain diagnosis here, other than the fact that you are in excellent physical condition, but if something is hurting you or causing these cramps of yours, I would recommend that you stop doing it."

Chris was not amused. He sensed what the doctor was about to say and hung his head in despair.

"Don't play baseball anymore and the cramps will probably go away. I know that's not what you wanted to hear, especially after chasing this thing for over two years, but that's all I've got for you."

We thanked the doctor for trying to help. I shook her hand and walked out. We were all extremely frustrated, though we were beginning to see that this was out of our hands.

Chris came to me later that week while I sat at the computer in my office again looking for a magic solution. He sat down on the sofa with tears in his eyes.

"Dad," he said, trying his best to hide his tears from me.

"What's going on, why the tears?"

Chris rubbed his eyes and admitted, "I think God wants me to leave baseball!" He hung his head as the tears finally appeared, flowing down his face. There was no holding them back now; the sport he had known and loved was slipping out of his reach and there was nothing he could do about it.

"Why would you say that, buddy?" I was shocked. I knew how much baseball meant to my son, and I couldn't believe that he would give it up. It had brought him so much joy through the years.

Chris inhaled and held his breath for a moment, collecting his thoughts. When he spoke, his words were slow. "Baseball has become my god. And I don't think God likes that. Doesn't it say something about that in the Bible?"

"Yes, of course. It's the very first of the Ten Commandments. I'd say it's pretty important to Him!"

Chris rested his head in my lap and cried. "I have to give it up," he sobbed. His words and sudden admission brought back a flood of memories of my son's baseball career. There were so many Little League games, tournaments, and high school games. Each one made me so proud. I thought back to when Chris first started to play baseball as a five-year-old. His initial joy in the game had never waned, even after all these years.

As I sat there doing my best to calm my son, I remembered a prayer I'd always prayed about each one of my children. I always asked God to open the doors my kids were supposed to go through and to close the doors they were not supposed to go through. All those Sunday mornings in church, escorting Chris to the altar to pray for relief from the cramps.

Thinking back on it, I'm sure God was frustrated with the situation too. He couldn't reveal His answer right now. We would all have to be patient and wait for God's plan for Chris's life to be revealed. But God did answer my prayer, even though I didn't agree with it. The door of baseball in Chris's life had been slowly closed. I knew that he was making the right decision in seeing that, but that didn't make it easy.

"I think you're doing the right thing," I whispered. "And I think you're doing it for the right reasons. I love you, buddy."

"I love you too, Dad," Chris said. "Thanks for all you've done, even the vinegar! I know it's been frustrating for you too. Anyway, I'm going to bed. Good night."

Chris got up and slowly walked away, hanging his head in disappointment.

"Good night," I said.

I sat in my dimly lit office thinking about the decision Chris had made and what impact this would have on his life. It was time for another talk with God. I lowered my head and folded my hands. I sat in silence for a few minutes thinking about what had just happened. So many thoughts were swirling in my head. I suddenly remembered how often I had asked God to help all my boys in their baseball careers. They were all good enough to get to the next level and excel. Chris had MLB scouts watching his games. I realized in that moment that I was being selfish. Maybe baseball had become my god too. I prayed for their success, but I wanted to be the dad of a big leaguer too. It was a wakeup call for me.

The Bible verse that popped into my head as I began to talk to Jesus is found in 1 Thessalonians 5:18: *Give thanks in all circumstances; for this is God's will for you in Christ Jesus.* I began to speak softly. "I know I've prayed for direction in Chris's life and I know he's doing what you want, following your will. But this one hurts."

I sat in silence again, longing to hear from God. After a few more minutes, I said, "Well, I'm just going to have to trust you on this one, Lord. I just ask that someday you'll show us that Chris has made the right choice."

CHAPTER 11
MIRACLES

Before I speak about some personal miracles in my life, I have to take a few minutes to explore the miracle of God's creation.

The concept of "small miracles" often refers to the intricate, awe-inspiring details in nature and the universe that seem to work together in perfect harmony. These phenomena, whether in the natural world, the human body, or the cosmos, often evoke a sense of wonder and point to the idea of a divine Creator. Here's a look at some examples of these "small miracles" and how they reflect the perfection and intentionality of creation:

The Human Body: Every cell in the human body contains DNA, a molecule that carries the genetic instructions for life. The complexity and precision of DNA are staggering—it contains about three billion base pairs in humans and yet it replicates itself with near-perfect accuracy. This intricate system allows for growth, healing, and the transmission of traits from one generation to the next. The fact that such a complex system works flawlessly is a testament to the brilliance of its design.

The Immune System: The immune system is a network of cells, tissues, and organs that work together to protect the body from harmful invaders like bacteria, viruses, and toxins. It can recognize and remember millions of different threats, adapting to fight them more effectively over time. The immune system's ability to distinguish between "self" and "non-self" and to mount a targeted response is a marvel of biological engineering.

The Eye: The human eye is an incredibly complex organ that can detect light, focus on objects near and far, and process millions of colors and shades. It works in tandem with the brain to create the images we see. The precision of the eye's design, from the lens to the retina, allows us to experience the beauty of the world in vivid detail.

Both of your eyes have six muscles that control movement. These muscles are how you can direct your eyes side-to-side, up and down, or at diagonal angles. The muscles that control eye movement all attach to the outside of your eyeball, which is why experts sometimes refer to them as "external" or "extrinsic" muscles.

While the external muscles mainly control which way your eyes point, they also play a role in how well you see. Your eyes need to move in ways that synchronize. If they don't, you won't be able to use certain visual capabilities like depth perception and three-dimensional (3D) vision.

Nature and God's Perfect Design: Photosynthesis could be a category all its own, but I'll include it here. Plants convert sunlight, carbon dioxide, and water into oxygen and glucose through photosynthesis. This process not only fuels the plant's growth but also produces the oxygen that humans and animals need to breathe.

The delicate balance between plants and animals, where each depends on the other for survival, reflects a beautifully orchestrated system.

Bees, butterflies, and other pollinators play a crucial role in the reproduction of many plants. As they collect nectar, they inadvertently transfer pollen from one flower to another, enabling fertilization. The mutualistic relationship between plants and pollinators ensures the survival of countless species and the production of fruits and seeds.

The Water Cycle: The water cycle, evaporation, condensation, precipitation, and collection, ensures that water is continuously recycled and distributed across the planet. This process sustains all forms of life. The self-sustaining nature of the water cycle demonstrates the perfect balance of Earth's ecosystems.

The Infinite Universe Cosmos: The laws of physics and the constants of nature, such as gravity, the speed of light, and the strength of atomic forces, are so precisely calibrated that even slight changes would completely alter life as we know it. This fine-tuning has led many to argue for the existence of an intelligent Designer. The fact that the universe is perfectly suited for life suggests a purposeful creation rather than random chance. I actually believe that the cosmos was designed by God to give us infinite destinations to explore once He remakes the planet. We're going to exist for eternity. We are going to need an infinite supply of new destinations to explore!

The Earth's Position: Some scientists call this the Goldilocks Zone. Earth is located not too close and not too far from the sun— allowing for the existence of liquid water, a key ingredient for life. The planet's tilt, rotation, and atmosphere also contribute to its habitability. The earth's unique conditions, from its distance from the sun to its magnetic field, make it a haven for life in an otherwise inhospitable universe.

Everyday Miracles (my personal favorite): Think about the complexity of the birth of a child. The development of a human being from a single fertilized cell into a fully formed baby is a process filled with wonder. Each stage of growth, from the formation of the heart to the development of the brain, is meticulously timed and executed. The miracle of life, repeated billions of times, is a testament to the creativity and care of the Creator.

The Changing Seasons: The earth's tilt and orbit around the sun create the cycle of seasons, each with its own beauty and purpose. Spring brings renewal, summer fosters growth, autumn prepares for rest, and winter allows for dormancy. The predictability and rhythm of the seasons reflect the order and intentionality of creation.

How It All Works Together: The harmony and interdependence of these systems suggest a level of design and intentionality that goes beyond random chance. From the microscopic world of DNA to the vastness of the cosmos, every detail seems to fit together like pieces of a grand puzzle. This interconnectedness points to the idea of a Creator who designed the universe with purpose and care.

For many, these "small miracles" are not just scientific phenomena but also spiritual reminders of God's presence and creativity. They invite us to pause, reflect, and marvel at the beauty and complexity of the world around us. As the psalmist wrote, "The heavens declare the glory of God; the skies proclaim the work of his hands" (Psalm 19:1). Whether through the intricacies of a cell or the vastness of the stars, creation speaks of a divine Artist whose work is both awe-inspiring and deeply personal.

❖ ❖ ❖

I have witnessed so many miracles in my life. Some small, some huge! The first that I remember was a really big one. It happened when I was about seventeen years old and still in high school. I attended Tokay High in Lodi and rode the bus to school every day. It wasn't something I enjoyed, but we lived about twenty miles from school and both my parents worked, so I had no other options. When my parents bought another car, my dad gave me his little Datsun (Datsun would become Nissan years later), but he didn't want me driving to school, so the dreaded bus trips continued. However, he allowed me to look for a job and gave me his blessing to use the car to get back and forth if I found something.

Within two days of that disclosure, I found a job as a busboy at Carmen's, a popular restaurant in Stockton. The drive to my new job took me down several country roads and put me on the road for a little over half an hour, but I didn't care. My new job meant financial freedom! So my new routine became school, home, change clothes, and go to my job. I worked from five until midnight, but there were times on the weekends when I worked until two o'clock in the morning. Looking back, I don't even know how I fit homework in, but I must have because I kept my grades up. That was something my parents insisted on.

The job was amazing! I cleared tables, helped the waitresses and bartenders, and the waitresses always shared their tips with me. Every night I left with anywhere from forty dollars up to a hundred bucks cash in my pocket! This was in the late '70s and made this high school kid feel like a lottery winner!

My new car, or new to me, had very small wheels. In fact, the wheels were only twelve inches. But being a typical kid with a little cash, I decided to make a few improvements. I bought some custom wheels and tires. I grew to love that little symbol of freedom. I even put a racing stripe on the hood! Over the next few months I started noticing that the car pulled a little to the left. I asked my dad what would cause this and he told me that I needed to get the wheels aligned. This would become my introduction to car maintenance. As it turns out, this also began my love/hate relationship with cars.

So in my free time I would stop by auto shops and ask if they could do a wheel alignment for me. It turns out that because my custom wheels were so small, shop after shop told me they couldn't help me because the machine that they used couldn't fit my tiny wheels. I went to five different shops over the next couple of weeks with no luck.

One Saturday night, as I was driving home after a very long shift, I fell asleep at the wheel as I approached a bridge. My grip on the steering wheel relaxed and the car pulled to the left. I hit the bridge on the passenger side of my car and I was jolted awake. It happened so fast that I never stopped driving. When I got home, I looked at the damage and it was pretty bad. The passenger side was scraped and covered in gray concrete dust. The back fender, bumper and taillight were damaged too. I went in and had to break the news to Mom and Dad. Needless to say, they weren't happy, but they were relieved that I wasn't injured.

The next day, I took the car to a body shop to find out how much it would cost to make the repairs. The guy at the shop looked at the damage and told me I was very lucky. He explained that if I had hit the bridge a few inches further to the right, the abutment would have hit the frame of my little car and it would have folded up like an accordion! He told me I would have certainly been killed. Immediately, I thought about all the time I spent looking for someone to align my wheels to keep it from pulling to the left. If I had had correctly aligned wheels, when I loosened my grip as I fell asleep, the car would not have pulled away from the bridge and I would not be here. God was already protecting me. I believe this was the first miracle He pulled off to keep me around to tell this story. Thank you, Jesus!

❖ ❖ ❖

When my son Chris decided on a college, he made up his mind pretty quickly that he wanted to attend California Baptist University in Riverside, California. Since my wife worked in a hospital, she knew very well the opportunities in the medical field and wanted our kids to have the best options available. She saw first-hand the monetary rewards and advancement opportunities for people working in a hospital every day. Our oldest son, Ben, had taken her advice and was now a nuclear medicine technologist, working in Irvine.

Both my wife and I had encouraged Chris to get into nursing. My wife had always said that he would be a great nurse. He had a soft, compassionate side while still remaining very competitive and both qualities would help in the life and career of nursing. She also knew that a man in a field dominated by females would have excellent chances of advancement and could probably get into management quickly should he choose that path.

So he decided on CBU and settled on nursing as his future. Until he made the decision, his major had still been undecided. We were excited for Chris once he settled on nursing. However, he didn't make that decision until one week before leaving for his freshman orientation. His financing was all settled and so were the majority of his first semester classes.

The decision to enter a career in nursing presented one small problem—CBU didn't offer a nursing program.

Not to be dispirited, the three of us had figured that Chris could attend his first year or two of college at CBU, and get the basic classes out of the way, while applying to schools that offered nursing programs. It would be a challenge, but we had faith and asked God to take Chris down the right path. The old prayer of asking God to open and close doors came rushing back. All those years of begging Him to take away the cramps. All those years of asking Him to let Chris get better so he could excel in baseball. Where was this all leading? I heard God whisper, "Have faith, Mike."

The next week, we loaded up our cars and made the trek to Riverside. The first thing that greeted us when pulling into the Cal Baptist parking lot was a very large banner hanging on one of the school buildings, which read, "Cal Baptist is proud to announce the brand-new Bachelor of Nursing program." This was extremely unexpected. *How did God do that?* I wondered. This was such an answer to our prayers that we could hardly believe it.

I read the sign and asked Chris, "So, do you think God wants you to be here?" It was obvious to us that God was in control of our lives and leading Chris by the hand. God finally revealed the plan for my son's life!

CHAPTER 12
GOD SPEAKS

Since my NDE, I've heard God speak several times in an audible voice. It is the same voice that I heard in the hospital both during my NDE and when Jesus spoke during my bout with pneumonia. I want to share some of those stories with you. Some of them are hard to believe, but some are downright amazing!

Here's an astonishing story of God speaking audibly to me and this one also has a crazy payoff!

❖ ❖ ❖

One Sunday morning, my wife and kids and I went to church, just like most Sundays. It was a beautiful, warm morning in the Central Valley. We had been attending this little church for a few years and we tried to go to church every weekend, but many times, our busy lives got in the way. This particular morning started as most did, all of us running a little late. But we managed to get out the door just in time.

We walked in just as the music started so no chitchat before service. We stood with the rest of the congregation and began singing the first hymn of Sunday morning worship. I looked around, silently thanking God for all the new friends in my life.

In a short two years, I had shared good times and bad times with this congregation. These people had been there for me and my family through it all. They had provided dinners while I battled that life-threatening illness a few years before. They were also supportive through Chris's injuries, offering prayers and words of wisdom. My friends in the congregation kept me focused on God and what was right with the world, instead of what was going wrong with mine. Our children had also made friendships that would last a lifetime in this church.

As we sang, the wife and young family of the youth pastor quietly snuck in and sat in the empty row in front of us. That's when I first heard the voice.

"Help them," someone said softly in my ear. It was quiet and, at first, I ignored it. I didn't recognize the voice, but after a moment those words were spoken again. "Help them."

I heard it several more times before I finally looked around and asked, "Help *who*?"

The voice gained clarity and now I heard it as if someone were standing right next to me, urging me. The voice said, "There is a need in this family and I want you to help them."

While the congregation kept singing, I sat down and prayed silently. "God, are you talking to me? I think I may be just hallucinating, or making this up in my mind, but if this is you, you know I will do whatever you ask, but you've got to be specific. Am I supposed to give them money?"

The voice said, "Yes."

I was floored. I took a deep breath and asked, "How much?"

The voice was silent. So I asked again, this time with a little bit more emphasis. "Please, how much?"

But the voice remained silent. I thought to myself, *Great*, thinking that I'd been left alone. But it was obvious. I knew that I had to do something. Was this really the voice of God? While it sounded familiar, at the same time it sounded different from the voice of Jesus that I had heard in the hospital. *Maybe this was actually God talking now, not Jesus*, I thought. *Even though they are one and the same, they're different, so they must have different voices!*

The church had a picnic scheduled for later that afternoon. So I decided to go home, ask God to be a little more specific, get some money, and give it to the family at the gathering. As church was dismissed, I walked out, praying. I grabbed my wife by the hand and hurried across the parking lot, toward the car.

As we rushed to the car, my wife asked, "Mike, what's going on? Are you in some kind of hurry? Is there a game on or something?" I just kept walking and she asked again, "Mike, are you okay?"

Just then I saw my kids across the parking lot looking for us. I waved at them, motioning for them to come to the car quickly.

I sat down in the driver seat, started the engine, and looked at my wife as the kids climbed into the back seat. With tears slowly forming in my eyes, I tried to put the words together to explain.

"God just told me to give some money to the pastor's family. As they were taking their seats in front of us, God spoke to me. Apparently there is some sort of need," I whispered.

My family sat in stunned silence. I didn't speak again but pulled out of the parking lot and headed home, trying not to cry. I'm a very emotional guy, though I try my best to hide it. Showing emotion to anyone, especially tears, was not something I was used to. I had grown up in a house where my father always told me to "be tough and act like a man." Crying was not something my father would consider manly. That could just be the cop in him! I didn't like feeling this vulnerable, but things like this didn't happen all the time. I had talked to God plenty of times, especially since the near-death experience, but He had not talked back to me since then.

When we got home, I headed upstairs to my bedroom, closed the door, and knelt next to my bed. I folded my hands, closed my eyes, and rested my forehead on my mattress. I thought for quite a while about what to say.

"Lord, thank you for talking to me today." God had actually spoken to me again, and I didn't know how to take it. "I feel overwhelmed that you would do that, and I'm amazed that I could hear you! I've been anxiously waiting to hear from you. I'm going to do what you ask, but I need help… I need to know how much to give them. I can't just give them a blank check or hand them a few bucks and say it's from you! It has to be the *right* amount! So if you would, please, tell me how much! If there's a need, I have to be sure to cover it."

I paused, reflecting on what I had just asked, and finished, "Amen."

I lifted my head off the bed, thought for a moment, and then quickly bowed my head again and said, "Oh, and Lord, thanks again for caring enough to ask me to do this for you. I promise I'll do the best I can. Amen."

I stood up and went back downstairs and found my wife in the kitchen, packing our lunch for the picnic.

She asked, "Do you know how much you're supposed to give them?"

"Well, not exactly. You can only get so much from an ATM at once, so I hope it's not going to be *too* much. I'm just going to have to wait and see. I prayed about it, but I haven't heard yet. I'm really afraid that if I don't know, and I make something up, it will be the wrong amount."

"Mike," she said, "this is God you're talking about. He will let you know."

"I sure hope so!"

"Well, either way, we'd better get going. We need to stop by and pick up my mom. I told her that it would be good for her to go with us; get her out of the house for a bit."

My wife's mother lived a few miles away. She was eighty-five years old and had symptoms of Alzheimer's disease, although no official diagnosis had been made yet. We both knew, though, that it was only a matter of time.

Mental disease is prevalent on my wife's side of the family. Her aunt had died a few years before from Alzheimer's. I knew that we needed to spend as much time as we could with her mom because she was showing all the classic signs. We knew it wouldn't be long before we had to move her into a home with full-time nursing care. If she had Alzheimer's, it also wouldn't be long before she stopped recognizing any of us at all. With that in mind, I was happy to take her places whenever we could.

We grabbed the lunch basket, blanket, and a few folding chairs and were off. While I drove, I began to silently pray again. "Lord, I'm on my way to the picnic and I haven't heard from you yet... I'm a little scared."

As my mother-in-law came walking out toward the car, I considered the coming scene; things would go one of two ways, I knew. She would either climb in with a familiar hello or get in the car and sit down quietly, looking around for something familiar.

I got out and opened the car door for her. "Hello, Michael," she said with a smile.

Feeling somewhat relieved, I replied, "Hi, ready for a picnic?" I was happy when I realized that today was a good day for her. She was well aware of her surroundings, which meant that we might just have a fun time at the picnic.

She nodded as I helped her into the back seat, buckled her seatbelt, and closed the door. I backed slowly out of the driveway and we made our way through her neighborhood into town. I made a quick stop at a grocery store around the corner from the church and walked up to the ATM inside the front door. I was still unsure of how much I was supposed to give. Was I missing something? What if God had already told me how much money to give to the pastor's family and I just hadn't heard it? Doubt started creeping into my mind.

This is stupid, I thought. *Maybe I should forget the whole thing. Maybe I didn't really hear that voice this morning. Maybe I just imagined it.*

I put my ATM card into the machine, though, and said out loud, "Come on, Lord!" Suddenly I felt as if I were under attack. I remembered the words of Jesus in the hospital. "When you step out in faith, the devil steps up his attack." Those voices of doubt were back and they echoed in my mind. I imagined a spiritual battle, good versus evil, being waged in the heavens above, but I tried to stay cool.

Of course I had heard the voice! And I was going to do this, no matter how stupid I felt. I suddenly felt compelled to withdraw $200, the maximum amount allowed by this particular ATM, all the time hoping that this was pleasing to God. Before I left, I walked to the greeting card section and picked up a card. It simply said "Friends" on the front. *This should work*, I thought.

Once back in the car, I wrote inside the card. "God asked me to give this to you. I'm not sure why, but there must be a need. And just in case there's not, keep it as a thank you for all you've done for my family. You bless us more than you know. We love you."

As I was writing in the card, my wife was telling her mom about the voice I had heard in church that morning. My mother-in-law grabbed her purse, reached into her wallet, and pulled out a twenty dollar bill, which she held up to me in the front seat.

"I want to help too!" she said, smiling.

I smiled back but insisted that this was between me and God. "You keep your money. If God wants you to give it away, He'll tell you!"

"Well," she said with excitement in her voice, "how do you know He didn't?"

I was a little perplexed at the clarity of her thought process. I had always heard God worked in mysterious ways, but this would be more than mysterious. This would just be weird!

Reluctantly, I said, "OK, I'll add your $20 to mine. It will be a kind of strange amount, but... whatever!" I was in no mood to argue. Besides, what if God really *did* want that extra $20 in there?

With that, I stuffed the money into the card and sealed it up.

"Two hundred and twenty dollars." I chuckled to myself. "It *is* a crazy amount."

❖ ❖ ❖

I don't usually answer my phone after dinner, but I was expecting our pastor to call. I wasn't able to speak with him at the picnic. Instead of handing the card to him, I opted to give it to his wife. The poor guy was in the dunk tank all afternoon with kids lining up to drop him into the cold water. He was a really good sport! But when my phone rang, I knew who it was, so I answered quickly.

"Hello," I said. There was only silence. I knew this was the moment when I would find out if I had followed God's command and if it was, in fact, God speaking to me that morning.

Finally there was a very quiet whisper on the other end of the phone. "Mike?" was all he asked.

I answered, "Yes, this is Mike."

Another silent pause followed. "Mike, it's me." I recognized the voice. It was my pastor, but he sounded upset. I thought, *Great, I made him cry. Maybe he took my gesture all wrong. Did I offend him?* I wondered.

"My wife gave me the card a few minutes ago. She said to tell you she was sorry, she completely forgot about it until just now."

I looked at my watch. It was almost nine o'clock.

"I don't know what to say," he said, followed by another long pause.

I let doubt creep back in and began to feel like a complete idiot again.

While I was busy feeling stupid and allowing all those negative thoughts to enter my mind, my pastor kept talking.

"Mike…" His voice cracked and I heard him take a deep breath. "It's unbelievable." I heard a few sniffles and realized he had been crying. "We had a flat tire today and my wife took the van to the tire shop. They told us we needed four new tires immediately. They also told us not to drive the van anymore until the tires were replaced. They are so badly worn that it made driving dangerous! But Mike, we didn't have the money and we didn't know what we were going to do. And then tonight I opened your card and almost fainted. Do you know how much the tires are going to be, Mike?"

Now I started choking back tears. "How much?" I asked.

"The guy at the shop said he had some great used tires he could put on the van for two hundred and twenty dollars, Mike…" He paused again and I could hear him taking a deep breath. "That's exactly how much you gave us. I just can't believe it. What a blessing! Thank you, Mike, thank you. I love you, brother!"

I was stunned. While I was telling him "You're welcome," I was thinking, *Thank you, Jesus*!

I was also thinking about that strange amount of money. I had been almost embarrassed when my mother-in-law added that extra $20. Now it seemed as if God knew just how much the family was going to need. This was certainly confirmation from God that I had not only done the right thing but that it really was God who had been talking that day. I couldn't believe it. God had really spoken to me! I was overwhelmed by the whole experience.

I hung up, dazed, and walked into my office. "What a day!" I folded my hands and thanked Jesus one more time for this miracle. I also thanked Him for speaking to me. *Incredible*, I thought. *God actually spoke to me. I'd been waiting patiently to hear from Him again!*

This is where the story gets even harder to believe. While sitting in my office, I noticed a stack of mail on my desk. My wife would sometimes put any mail addressed to me on the desk. I picked up the envelopes and sorted through them. One of them caught my eye. It was from a friend of mine who I had done some work for a couple months ago. He was building a new house and asked me to paint it for him. I had spent a few years as a licensed painting contractor in California, so I was happy to help. Of course he offered to pay me and we had the usual argument between friends. "Just pay for the materials," I told him. But he insisted on paying for my time. I didn't put up much of a fight because I knew it would take quite a bit of time, especially only working weekends and squeezing out any little bit of free time. I had finished the job a few weeks before and now he had sent me a note and a check. When I saw the amount that he paid me, it took my breath away. He sent a check for $2200.

As I thought about the amount, I said it a few times in my head, trying to figure out why it had struck my attention and then suddenly remembered the money God had told me to give to my pastor. That odd amount of $220. My knees got weak.

I suddenly realized that the amount I had given to the pastor's family was exactly ten percent of the check I just received, to the penny! Was this God's way of saying thank you? Or was it His way of acknowledging that I had done the right thing? Of course it was. It was both of those things and more! I had more confirmation from God. I had tithed on an amount I had not even received yet! I had done the right thing and I knew for certain that the message—that voice I had heard in church—had come from God Himself. It was as if God was thanking me for trusting Him.

I grabbed my Bible from the table next to my desk and opened it to a passage in Deuteronomy that said, "All these blessings shall come upon you and overtake you, if you obey the voice of the Lord your God." I was sure that God had sent this check as a blessing for listening and obeying. I should say that I'm not a fan of playing

Bible roulette, but God surely opened my Bible for me. He wanted me to read that passage at that exact moment.

It wasn't the first time the Lord had shown me the way. Here's another exciting story with just as amazing an ending.

❖ ❖ ❖

My wife and I attended a church fundraiser one Sunday night. When we walked into the room, it was already very crowded. We stood at the door looking for a couple of open seats and found a few next to our friends. This particular friend happened to be the first guy who greeted me the very first time we walked into that little country church. He was a San Francisco Giants fan, so we hit it off immediately.

"What's up, Mike?" my friend asked as I sat down. He was such a good man and always excited to see me. Within minutes the conversation turned to the Giants, as it always did between us.

An air of excitement filled the hall during dinner as word began to spread that the church was going to launch a brand-new program that night. It was the brainchild of Donny Lambert, a retired pharmacist who had attended the church for over forty years. Donny had spent the last ten years going on mission trips around the world. He had a great sense of humor and loved talking to strangers about Jesus. Donny's campaigns for the church were always very exciting and everyone anticipated hearing from him.

Within minutes of finishing my meal, Donny made his way to the stage to address the crowd. As he did, the doors in the back of the room burst open with a bang. Everyone turned to see what the noise was all about.

Through the doors came a small school bus, about six feet long, made of large sheets of cardboard and painted yellow. There were eight crudely cut windows on each side and a large hole in the front representing the windshield. The bus followed Donny's footsteps toward the stage. A young man was inside the contraption, holding it on his shoulders as he walked.

Just before he arrived at the stage, the young man "driving" the bus stumbled and the front of the bus gripped the carpet, causing it to stop abruptly. We could all hear giggles coming from inside the cardboard bus as the young man picked it up and moved a few more feet before setting the bus down. As he lowered his body to the ground inside the bus he started laughing as he thought about his misstep. This led the audience to laugh along with him.

Donny asked for everyone's attention and began to explain his plan. "I want to introduce you to our latest program for summer camp." He told us that he envisioned the church sponsoring children who lived nearby to go to their summer camp. His idea was for members of the church to pay for kids from the surrounding neighborhoods to go to camp at a cost of $50 per child. The camp was held for one week each year in mid-July and accepted kids aged eight to twelve. The sponsored kids would spend a week at camp and when they came back, the hope was that the parents would start attending the church. By reaching kids for Jesus, Donny hoped to eventually bring their entire families to know Christ as well.

It sounded like an excellent idea to me. As Donny was on stage explaining his program, I heard a voice behind me, but very close, say, "I want you to give one thousand dollars."

I turned to reply, expecting to see one of my buddies whispering in my ear. I asked out loud, "What?"

The voice again said, "I want you to give one thousand dollars."

As I turned to the other side, I said, "I don't have a thousand dollars to give!" I was shocked when I found that no one was standing on the other side of me either. There was certainly no one close enough to have whispered in my ear.

My wife heard me reply and asked, "What?"

I was feeling somewhat shaken, so I looked at her and asked, "What?"

She was confused. "You said something. I didn't hear you and asked you what you said."

I suddenly recognized this voice. It was the voice of God! It was the same voice that had told me to give money to our pastor and his family.

I had prayed for a long time to hear from God again, but until now He had remained silent. I missed hearing from Him. I'd had moments where I sat in silence for hours asking God to speak to me again; most of the time I figured that He was busy with other, more important, things and didn't have time to talk to me. *This must be important to God if He's talking to me again,* I thought.

I got up, excused myself from the table, and walked out to my car. I sat in the driver's seat and closed my eyes, trying to gather my thoughts.

Finally I rested my head on the steering wheel and said, "Lord, I don't have an extra thousand dollars lying around right now. I don't know how I can do this. As I'm sure you know, we've had our share of unexpected bills lately and things are just a little tight right now!"

God said, "You'll get it back!"

I opened my eyes and looked straight ahead, out the windshield. I almost expected to see someone standing in front of me holding out a handful of money.

But I'd been through this before. For some reason, He was back and He had another very specific mission in mind. I knew I couldn't say no to God; this had to be very important for Him to finally break His silence with me. But how could I say yes when I knew that it was beyond my means? Still, it had been over a year since I first heard that voice. It had told me to do the right thing before and now it seemed that He had a new assignment! There was no other choice; I had to find a way to give $1000. I knew that the money would pay for twenty kids to go to camp and spend two weeks getting to know Jesus. The eternal implications were profound. When I thought about it, I realized that it was a very worthwhile cause.

"OK, God, I'm going to trust you. I'll write the check," I said quietly. I got out of the car and started walking back to the meeting. On my way back in, I saw my friend Bill.

"Bill!" I yelled across the parking lot.

Bill turned and waved when he saw me. "Hey, Mike! I wondered where you went. I came out looking for you!" He changed direction and the two of us met near the edge of the parking lot.

"It happened again!"

"What happened, Mike?"

"God spoke to me again. I heard Him again!" I was really excited and anxious to share this revelation with my friend. Bill looked at me, confused, and I continued. "Remember I told you how I heard God that one time and He asked me to give money to the pastor?"

Bill nodded. "Oh yeah. That was pretty freaky!"

"Well, He just asked me to give a thousand dollars to this summer camp thing."

"No shit!" Bill didn't normally use that kind of language and quickly offered an apology. Then he asked, "What did He say, exactly?"

"He said, 'I want you to give one thousand dollars,' and that I'd get it back!"

"Really! So are you going to do it?"

"Yes, of course! I have nothing to lose! He said I'd get it back! And I'm not about to say no to God."

Bill looked a little puzzled. "I don't want to rain on your parade here, Mike, but are you sure it was God?"

I thought for a moment. It had to be—it was the same voice I'd heard before, the same voice I'd heard in church, and it was the same voice I'd heard in the hospital. It was definitely the voice of Jesus, I was certain. "I'm positive. I just got my checkbook and I'm going in there to write a check right now. Hey, here's a wild idea; why don't you do the same? Donny said they wanted to raise five thousand dollars so they could send a hundred kids to camp. That would make them closer to their goal, all in the first night! I bet Donny would be pretty surprised!"

Bill smiled. "You think God wanted you to tell me so I'd write a check too?"

"Ok, I don't know, but maybe! I mean, why not?" I thought for a moment.

Bill continued his in-depth analysis of the situation. "Of course, God knows how this is all going to play out, right? I mean, He knows that you're giving the money and now, because of you giving, I'm going to give some too. He knows that I would take this as a challenge. Sounds to me like God is an efficiency expert! He knows how to get a real bang for the buck! Alright, my friend, I'll write a check too, for one thousand dollars. Furthermore, I'm going to go into the meeting and tell everyone what you heard and what I'm doing about it. Then I'm going to issue a challenge to the entire congregation! Let's send some kids to camp!"

We walked back into the church hall and dropped our checks into a box that Donny had conveniently placed on a tall table on stage. And true to his form, Bill grabbed the microphone and issued his challenge to the congregation. And there were actually quite a few people who came up and dropped their checks into the box. It was a very fun evening and we raised a lot of money!

The next day, I came home from work for a quick lunch. My house was one of the first ones completed in the first phase of the new neighborhood I was in charge of building. I sat down at the computer in my office and logged on to my online stock account. I had been an amateur day-trader for a few years. I had done pretty well and loved the thrill of trading stocks. I would buy and hold most stocks for a day or two, sometimes a week. I was a small-time trader who was happy if I had any type of positive gain at the end of the month! My expectations were very low! I had gotten pretty good at recognizing the right economic indicators and used that to my advantage when trading.

Every once in a while, I would hear about a stock or see it mentioned in a business magazine and would buy shares on a whim. So this particular afternoon, I sat down and logged in to my online trading account. I was shocked when I saw the total amount on the homepage. Apparently one of the stocks I had bought the previous week made a huge move. The value of my account had risen one thousand dollars just that morning! I searched through my portfolio and identified which stock had suddenly jumped. I quickly sold the stock and, within a few minutes, the money was added to the cash account instead of just being listed as an asset. I sat there stunned. Before logging out, I heard that voice echo in my thoughts. *"You'll get it back!"*

I paused, swallowing heavily. I had just made my $1000 back, just like God had told me! Once again, God had proven to me that He was completely in charge, and since I was obedient, God had kept His word.

I bowed my head and closed my eyes, this time more over-whelmed than just moments ago. I felt so humbled by this dramatic series of events and witnessing God's power but felt that it wasn't enough to just bow my head and close my eyes. I felt a need to show God just how much I revered Him. I slid out of my chair, got on my knees on the floor, and started praying. The power of the Lord showered down on me like a ton of bricks and I began to cry.

"Thank you, Lord, you are so true to your word. You are truly in charge of everything!" I lay on the floor, quietly weeping and in awe of what had just happened. *God is so good*, I thought. *So good*.

❖ ❖ ❖

About ten years after my near-death experience, I was offered a job with a major paint company as an outside sales representative selling their product. With my background in construction and paint in particular, I thought it would be a good opportunity. They gave me a new territory and assigned $800,000 worth of business in a brand-new territory. In six months I turned that 800 grand into $1.6 million. So things were going very well!

But this company didn't have the greatest delivery system. A lot of the paint that I sold had to be delivered on pallets from our factory in Thousand Oaks, California by a third party. We happened to use FedEx for the larger, bulkier supplies that would be delivered to my contractors and their job sites.

One late summer afternoon, I was waiting on a delivery alongside several workers from one of my customer's teams. The delivery was running behind and his guys told me they would have to leave soon. I told them I would wait for the delivery, sign for it, and secure it inside the garage, and afterwards I would lock up the house so they would be able to go home on time. The delivery got there much later than any of us anticipated, so I was all alone when it finally arrived. I unloaded the pallet, grabbing two 5-gallon cans of paint at a time and walking them into the garage. As I turned with the last two buckets, I spun around and stepped in a rather large hole. The driveway wasn't paved yet, so I fell quite a ways below where I should have stepped. I heard my knee pop and down I went. I knew from the pain shooting down my leg that this was a pretty bad injury. I did my best to secure the house and eventually got it locked up. I limped back to my car and tried calling my boss. He didn't answer so I sent an email and told him I would need to seek medical attention first thing in the morning.

The next day, the early diagnosis from the doctor wasn't good as he examined my swollen knee. He sent me to get an MRI and that news was even worse than I thought. It turned out I had something called a "horseshoe" tear in my meniscus and another smaller tear on the other side of my knee. There was also damage to the kneecap and surrounding tendons. Surgery was in my near future. I ended up having three surgeries over the next year and a half. This injury was covered by worker's compensation since it happened on the job.

A few months after the third surgery, I was sitting at home and I heard God say to me, "Big changes are coming."

I sat up and spoke back. "What?"

The voice said again, "Big changes are coming."

I said, "God, what do you mean?"

Now, you may be wondering how I knew this was God. Here is the simple explanation. When God speaks audibly to you, you will know. Besides, I was alone in the house and it could only have been God! And yes, it was the same voice I had heard several times before. Only this time, the voice had me shaking. So I asked again, "What changes?" There was no answer. So I asked, "Will they be good changes or bad?"

God answered, "They will be bad temporarily, but they will be good in the long run." The voice was so crystal clear that I came home and recorded a video to myself on my iPhone so I would remember the date and time and exactly what was said.

The next day, I opened the mail and there was a letter from the disability office saying we had made a mistake on our taxes. It went on to explain that I had shown too much income and would not be eligible for any more disability payments if I was able to earn income! So I called our accountant and explained the situation to him. Apparently some of my wife's income from her business was listed as both of ours. It was a simple clerical error, but it was frightening! So our accountant had to file an amended return. So big changes were bad, but only temporarily, just as God had promised.

A few weeks later, the disability office contacted me and said they accepted the amended return. Changes were good in the long run! I was eventually able to get off disability, but I left the paint company.

I don't want you to think that God speaks like that all the time. But I wish He would!

CHAPTER 13
LIFE AFTER MY NDE

After I left the hospital, everything changed. And not all the changes were easy or good. The best thing that happened to me had to do with my prayer life. But first and foremost, I have learned to read my Bible every day. I'm still human, so there are times when I forget, or get too busy, but it is a way of life now.

Every morning, before the world wakes up, I carve out a few moments to allow God to speak to me through the pages of His Word. It's my sacred time, my daily appointment with God. I've learned that the best way to hear His voice is through His Word, so I open my Bible and let the pages speak to me. It's not just a habit—it's the heartbeat of my day.

I remember when I first started this routine. Life was noisy, chaotic, and I often felt like I was drowning in my own thoughts. I'd pray, but it felt one-sided, like I was talking into the void. Then someone told me, "If you want to hear God, read His Word. That's how He speaks to us." So I decided to give it a try.

At first, it felt a little awkward. I wasn't sure where to start or what to expect. But I began with the Psalms and something about the honesty and beauty of those words resonated with me. David's cries for help, his songs of praise, his raw emotions—it felt like he was putting my own heart into words. And through those verses, I started to hear God's voice, gentle and clear, reminding me that He was with me.

Now it's become the most important part of my day. I wake up early, make a cup of coffee, and sit in my favorite chair by the window. Other times, I sit up in bed with my dogs fighting for the prime lap position. The house is quiet, the world outside still soft with the morning light. I open my Bible and it's like stepping into a conversation with God. Some days, a verse jumps out at me, speaking directly to something I'm going through. Other days, it's a story or a teaching that challenges me to grow. But every time, without fail, I feel His presence.

There was one morning I'll never forget. I was feeling overwhelmed, unsure about a decision I needed to make. I opened my Bible to Proverbs and my eyes landed on Proverbs 3:5–6: "Trust in the Lord with all your heart and lean not on your own understanding; in all your ways submit to Him, and He will make your paths straight." It was like God was sitting right there with me, saying, "I've got this. Trust Me." Tears filled my eyes as I realized how personal and loving His guidance is.

Reading the Bible daily has changed everything for me. It's not just about gaining knowledge or checking off a spiritual to-do list. It's about relationship. It's about hearing God's voice, feeling His love, and learning to walk in His ways. Some days, the words comfort me. Other days, they convict me. But every day, they draw me closer to Him.

I've come to see my Bible as more than a book; it's a guide. And every morning, when I open it, I'm reminded that God is speaking. All I have to do is listen.

❖ ❖ ❖

Since my near-death experience I talk to God all day! As I'm working around my house I talk to Him. When I'm mowing the lawn, I talk to Him. When I'm taking a walk, I talk to Him. I'm constantly talking to Him, and when I do, I now visualize His face. I remember our conversation in the hospital and it makes me smile. I can picture his facial expressions too. It's like we do life together now. And it's not just me who does all the talking. Jesus is with me all the time and I can recognize His presence.

One time, while I was doing some work on my property, I needed a nail gun. I was building a shed at the new house we had just purchased. There was literally no storage for any of my equipment, and I've got a lot of tools that needed a home! So I poured a foundation for a twelve-by-twelve outbuilding and bought all the lumber that I needed for the walls. When I fired up my air compressor and attached my nail gun, I realized it was toast. So it was time to head to the hardware store and grab a nail gun. I bought one, brought it home, and hooked it up to my air compressor. I was about to use it for the first time when I noticed a big warning tag hanging from the handle. It said, "Warning, using this nail gun without adding oil voids the warranty."

I had never heard of such a thing! I realized that maybe that's why the old nail gun seized up and died. So I did a Google search and found that you do indeed need to add oil to any nail gun. The problem was I was ready to start building walls, but I didn't have any oil. And this wasn't just any oil. It was very specific. It had to be "air tool oil." So I started looking through my toolbox figuring I had to have some air tool oil somewhere, but after looking around for a long time, I came up empty. That's when I decided to get Jesus involved. I sat down on an old five-gallon bucket and folded my hands. I said, "Lord, I'm going to keep this short and simple. I need some air tool oil. Can you help me?" I heard His answer in my spirit. Jesus chuckled and thanked me for involving Him in the minutia of my life. He actually says that quite often to me. He told me to keep looking, so I did.

I went back to the top drawer of my toolbox where I first started my search. It was quite messy. After moving, I didn't take time to keep it as organized as I usually would. I found a small plastic bag that was pretty dusty. I opened the bag and looked inside. There was a very small, clear plastic bottle with a red cap on it. I pulled the bottle out and read the sticker that was on the side. It said, "Air tool oil." I was flabbergasted! Jesus had answered my prayer. Before I said thank you, I laughed because I realized it was probably the air tool oil that came with the last nail gun that I had just replaced. I had never used the oil and I'm certain that it was because of my carelessness that the old nail gun met an early demise!

I can honestly say that Jesus wants to be part of your life and longs for a close relationship with you. Try to include Him in everything, even if it seems too small to include Him. He loves it!

❖ ❖ ❖

Another change I have witnessed is I definitely notice the beauty around me more. When I watch a sunset or marvel at His creation, I talk to Him and sometimes I ask, "Where did you get the idea for that?" I don't take God's creation for granted anymore either. I do stop and smell the roses all the time. I do acknowledge the beauty of His creation now. And when I take pictures of His creation, I thank Him. There have been times when I have been staring at a sunset and simply said, "Thank you." I think He appreciates that. I've slowed my pace down enough to notice even the smallest miracles. Slow down and smell the roses. It's more than a cliché. It's a way of life.

❖ ❖ ❖

At the time of my NDE we were attending a Baptist Church in Manteca. It was a small church where everybody knew one another.

One day, during his sermon, our pastor told the church that he had had a vision from God and He wanted our small congregation to become a big church in our little town. He said the vision was for our church to become more like Saddleback Church in Southern California. His vision included building not only a new church but a missionary center from where we would send out missionaries to the world and spread the good news of Christ. It sounded great, so we all got to work. We put together a building committee to follow the pastor's vision. It was our job to plan the steps for the expansion of our campus. One of the members of our church donated some land on the edge of town, so that was taken care of. But next we had to submit our plans to the planning commission.

I was on the building committee along with about a dozen of my fellow parishioners. After our first meeting, one of the members of the building committee told us that he had been diagnosed with cancer. Before the next meeting one of our members announced that he was going through a divorce. A few weeks later, another member told us he was moving out of town and would need to step down as a member of the committee.

I remember talking to one of my friends and suggesting that we were under attack. I recommended that instead of meeting we should just get together and pray for the members of our church and specifically the members of our building committee. Ephesians 6:12 states, "For our struggle is not against flesh and blood, but against the rulers, against the authorities, against the powers of this world's darkness, and against the spiritual forces of evil in the heavenly realms."

It seemed like too much of a coincidence for so many members of our building committee to have major life changes so suddenly. I was convinced it was spiritual warfare.

I was the last board member to fall victim to the schemes of the evil one. After twenty-nine years of marriage, I too would be going through a divorce. The spiritual attacks had landed on my doorstep and there was no avoiding this. I've always heard that the devil attacks the effective Christian with more veracity. Jesus's prophecy was coming true, step by step. I remember telling my kids, "I can divorce your mother, but you can't." I encouraged my children to love and honor her like it says in the Ten Commandments. I knew God had a better plan for my life, but when you go through these things, it's hard to see the end while you're still walking down that difficult path. Looking back, I can see that it was the best thing for me. While I was living through this tumultuous time, I heard the words Jesus spoke to me very often. "You have some valleys to walk through. It is necessary. Remember, I will be with you and giving you courage."

Every time I recalled His voice and those words, I thought, *Okay, this is certainly a valley. Now, how about that encouragement you promised?* And as soon as that memory popped into my head, I was at peace.

❖ ❖ ❖

It was difficult for my family to go through a divorce, but it was inevitable. I think I was more worried about the impact it would have on my kids' lives than my own. I want to share this very personal story because I want you to know that bad things can happen to Christians too. You can do everything right in life and still have tragedy, but God will be with you and God will see you through it. I remembered the other revelation Jesus shared with me in the hospital. "When you step out in faith, the enemy steps up his attacks." He was right about that too. But even if you don't hear His voice, if you call on Him, He will comfort you.

That brings up a larger point that I want to explore. Why *do* bad things happen to God's children? It's a question you hear all the time and certainly one that I am asked constantly. The easy answer is that we all live in a sinful, fallen world. There's no escaping sin. When Adam and Eve defied God in the Garden of Eden, it affected all of mankind, forever. But I think there are many reasons and most can be found in Scripture. The Bible addresses the question of why suffering exists, even for those who love God. While it doesn't offer a single, simple answer, here are a few key passages that provide clarity and comfort:

In Genesis 3, the Bible teaches that suffering entered the world through human rebellion. Because of sin, creation is broken, and pain, injustice, and death affect everyone, righteous and unrighteous alike (Romans 8:20–22). Even those who love God are not exempt from the brokenness of this world. John 16:33 states, "In this world you will have trouble. But take heart! I have overcome the world."

God often uses trials to deepen trust in Him, refine character, and prepare believers for greater purposes. This is undoubtedly true in my life. Romans 5:3–5 puts it like this: "We glory in our sufferings, because we know that suffering produces perseverance; perseverance, character; and character, hope." James 1:2–4 adds, "Consider it pure joy when you face trials of many kinds, because the testing of your faith produces perseverance."

I often think of the time when Jesus was preparing me to that of Job in the Bible. While I didn't suffer near the tragedy that Job did, I've asked myself more than once, "Am I a modern-day Job?" The story of Job emphasizes that God's wisdom and sovereignty transcend human comprehension. Job, a righteous man, endures immense suffering, yet God never fully explains "why." Instead, He reveals His authority over creation and calls Job to trust Him. Proverbs 3:5–6 further reminds us to "Trust in the Lord with all your heart, and lean not on your own understanding."

Many times God uses suffering to cause us to cry out to Him. Let's face it; some of us are very reluctant to lean on someone other than ourselves. I think men may be more susceptible to that line of thinking because we are very independent. That was certainly my case. But God has a way of bringing us to our knees in time of need and desperation. When we are on our knees, the natural thing to do is pray. It's always alright to cry out to God and it's never too late.

The Bible consistently shows God bringing good out of evil. Joseph, betrayed and enslaved, later says in Genesis 50:20, "You intended to harm me, but God intended it for good to accomplish what is now being done."

The Bible acknowledges the mystery of suffering while affirming God's goodness. It invites us to lament (Psalm 22, Psalm 13) and ask hard questions, yet also to trust that God is present in our pain and working for our ultimate redemption. Jesus Himself, innocent and sinless, suffered profoundly, showing that God does not stand aloof from human pain but enters into it.

The Bible never promises a pain-free life for those who love God, but it assures us that suffering is not meaningless; God is with us (Psalm 23:4) and His purposes will prevail.

So God uses the valleys in our lives to create a need for Him and a reason to call on Him. Is that cruel? If you realize that we were made to live forever, and forever is a long time, it helps add perspective. This life that we are living now will be just a blip on the radar of our lifetime. Will I remember a hundred thousand years from now that I went through a time of betrayal? I don't think so. And it won't even matter! I have forgiven people who wronged me. I'll admit it's not easy. Let me expand on that thought too.

When I discovered trouble in my marriage, many of my friends turned their backs on me. There were lies told about me and lots of gossip. It hurt. And none of my Christian friends handled that tumultuous time as the Bible instructs. I can't say I blame them because it's easy to do, or not do, depending on your perspective.

But I can honestly say that I felt Jesus the entire time. He never let me go. He cried with me. He helped me back up and helped me to start over. His words echoed in my ears many times during my traumatic season, just like He told me in the hospital. It's not an easy thing to start over at age forty-eight. But I did. And I did it with the love and guidance of Jesus.

I met my current wife, Melissa, and I've dedicated this book to her. As it says in the dedication, "I now know what it's like to be truly loved." Jesus knew the happy ending I was in store for. And now we smile together.

❖ ❖ ❖

Another life lesson from my NDE is that I pray all the time. I started something that may seem odd to some people, but I learned to give myself a gentle reminder. There's a saying that's always stuck with me: "Idle hands are the devil's workshop." I'm not sure where I first heard it, but it's become a guiding principle in my life. I've always believed that staying purposeful and focused is key to living a life of faith and joy. But, like anyone, I have moments of boredom when my mind starts to wander and I feel that restless pull toward distraction.

One day, I was sitting in the park, waiting for a friend. The sun was warm and the breeze gentle, but I found myself fidgeting, my hands restless and my thoughts scattered. That's when I remembered the "idle hands" saying. I decided to try something simple: I folded my hands in my lap, as if in prayer. Almost instantly, I felt a sense of calm wash over me. It was like my folded hands became a physical reminder to focus on Jesus, to turn my thoughts toward gratitude and faith.

From that day on, folding my hands became my go-to move whenever I felt bored or restless. Waiting in line at the grocery store? Folded hands. Sitting in a quiet room with nothing to do? Folded hands. It became a habit; a small but powerful way to stay grounded and connected to my faith. Even in the busiest or most mundane moments, those folded hands were like a silent prayer, keeping my heart and mind focused on what truly mattered.

But there were times when folding my hands wasn't possible— like when I was walking with the dogs. In moments when folding my hands wasn't practical I found another way to stay focused. I'd lift my hands slightly, as if in praise, and let my heart fill with gratitude. It didn't matter if I was alone or in a crowd; this small act became my way of celebrating my faith and refocusing my mind.

Over time, people started to notice. Friends would ask why I always seemed so calm, even in the busiest moments. I'd smile and say, "Idle hands may be the devil's workshop, but folded hands are a prayer and lifted hands are a song of praise." It wasn't anything grand or dramatic, just a simple practice that kept me connected to Jesus.

Now it's just part of who I am. Whether I'm folding my hands or lifting them in praise, I've found a way to turn even the quietest, most ordinary moments into something meaningful. And in those moments, I feel closer to God than ever.

One other benefit of folding my hands is the fact that I can't hold my phone with folded hands. Talk about the devil throwing me a distraction! So when I set my phone down and fold my hands, I think, *Not today, Satan!*

❖ ❖ ❖

Halfway through writing this book, I encountered something inexplicable. It was a chilling echo of the words Jesus had spoken to me years earlier in the hospital. "When you step out in faith, the enemy steps up his attack."

One night, I experienced something that sounds straight out of a horror movie; I was attacked by demons. I had fallen asleep on the couch and Melissa had chosen to throw a blanket over me and let me sleep undisturbed. It started around 2:00 a.m. with what I assumed was just a nightmare.

In the dream, I walked into a house we had renovated only to find the back door sealed shut by a brick wall. Suddenly, the walls began closing in. Then two shadowy figures appeared, towering over me like slabs of very tall, thin and soaking wet cardboard. They crept closer, and in a surge of panic, I shouted, "Leave in the name of Jesus!" My words were somewhat garbled as I was still asleep. But one of the demons understood my muttered words and he vanished instantly. I yelled again, jolting myself awake, but the other lingered.

Even as I lay fully conscious on the couch, their sinister presence clung to the air. I felt a cold grip seize me from behind. When I glanced down, gnarled, root-like arms stretched across my chest, coiling toward my legs. I cried out once more, invoking the name of Jesus, and the creature dissolved. Shaken, I stumbled to bed after a hurried prayer.

But hours later, I sensed its return—a creeping dread in the dark. I commanded it to leave and it obeyed.

Stranger still were the eerie clues left behind: the refrigerator's motion-sensor light glowed inexplicably, though our cat slept soundly in the bedroom. Even my dog, who always burrows under the covers, stayed alert beside me, staring intently at the door as if on guard.

I can't shake the feeling that God is pulling back a veil, letting me glimpse the unseen spiritual battleground around us. Jesus warned me. Even with the warning Jesus gave me, I was frightened.

The following day, after receiving advice from a dear friend, I walked around every inch of my home and property claiming sacred ground and exorcising any demons. I'm happy to report that it was a successful "exorcism" and my property is demon-free. Whatever you encounter in this world, it cannot withstand the name of Jesus.

There are many verses in the Bible that tell of Jesus casting out demons. My favorite is found in Mark 1:34: "And he healed many who were ill with various diseases, and cast out many demons; and he was not permitting the demons to speak, because they knew who he was." I love this because this verse makes it clear that demons must obey Jesus.

And this leads me to another Bible verse. John 14:12–14 states, "Very truly I tell you, whoever believes in me will do the works I have been doing, and they will do even greater things than these, because I am going to the Father. And I will do whatever you ask in my name, so that the Father may be glorified in the Son. You may ask me for anything in my name, and I will do it."

Don't miss the importance of the words of Jesus. We can and will do greater things. That's powerful! Jesus is saying that we have power over demons and I just proved it!

CHAPTER 14
FORTY YEARS

Jesus took forty years to answer my childhood prayer. God often uses waiting periods to prepare us for what's ahead. During these forty years, He may have been working in ways I couldn't see, shaping my character, deepening my curiosity of Him, and aligning circumstances for His perfect plan for my life.

The number forty holds deep spiritual meaning and my experience of waiting for four decades mirrors many significant biblical stories where God's timing, though often mysterious, proves to be perfect and transformative.

In the Bible, the number forty is deeply symbolic, representing periods of testing, preparation, transformation, and fulfillment. It often marks a time when God works in profound ways, even when His presence or plan isn't immediately visible. Here are some examples given to us in Scripture:

The first story is found in Numbers 14:33–34. After being freed from slavery in Egypt, the Israelites wandered in the wilderness for forty years.

This period was a consequence of their lack of faith and their disobedience, but it was also a time of refinement and preparation. God used those forty years to shape a new generation that would trust Him and enter the Promised Land. On the eve of their long-awaited entry into Canaan, God had Moses send out spies into the land so they could explore. They spent forty days and nights scouting the land before returning to report they had found nothing.

For me, looking back on my life, my forty-year wait felt like a wilderness season and at times a feeling of uncertainty and longing and even questioning. I've never felt at ease in this world. I've always known there was more, but couldn't put my finger on it. I've never felt like this world was home. Yet, just as God was with the Israelites, He was with me and has even led me to a more fulfilled life; a life dedicated to furthering His message of hope and bringing glory to Him and the Kingdom of God. He spent years shaping my heart and preparing me for the answer to my prayer.

In Acts 7:29–30, Moses spent forty years in the wilderness of Midian before God called him to lead the Israelites out of Egypt. Those years were not wasted; they were a time of preparation, where Moses learned humility, dependence on God, and the skills he would need for his mission. God called Moses to the top of Mt. Sinai for forty days and forty nights without eating bread or drinking water. There, God gave Moses His covenant, the Ten Commandments, so His people could live in alignment with the Lord.

Similarly, my forty-year wait may have been a time of hidden preparation, where God was equipping me for the moment when His answer would finally come.

Matthew 4:1–2 tells how Jesus fasted and prayed for forty days and forty nights in the wilderness, enduring temptation and drawing closer to the Father. This period of testing strengthened Him for His ministry. My forty-year wait may have felt like a spiritual battle at times, but it has also been an opportunity to grow in faith, perseverance, and reliance on God. After my NDE, God told me to wait on telling the second half of my experience. I had to endure thousands of comments from doubters and naysayers to prepare me to stand up and refute every single one of them.

In my favorite Bible story of David and Goliath, found in 1 Samuel 17:16, God's people had to endure taunting and challenges from Goliath before David was sent to the battlefield with bread for his brothers and decides he's the one who will fight Goliath.

When the prophet Elijah fled the wicked queen Jezebel, he traveled for forty days and nights until he reached Mount Horeb. 1 Kings 19:8 tells us that Elijah sheltered in a cave where he heard God speak to him in a gentle whisper.

As told in Acts 1:3, after His crucifixion and resurrection, Jesus remained and walked with His disciples for forty days and nights before ascending to Heaven.

So we see many stories in the Bible where the number forty often marks a transition from one season to another. Whether the actual number should be taken literally is what I call an in-house debate. For the Israelites, it was the transition from slavery to freedom; for Jesus, it was the transition from private life to public ministry. My forty-year wait has now culminated in a new season of fulfillment and blessing. The answer to my prayer carried even greater meaning because of the time I spent waiting and trusting. Forty years sounds like a long time to have a prayer answered, but let's not forget what the Word of God clearly states in 2 Peter 3:8: "But do not forget this one thing, dear friends: With the Lord a day is like a thousand years and a thousand years are like a day."

Throughout the Bible, God proves Himself faithful to those who wait on Him. The Israelites eventually entered the Promised Land, Moses fulfilled his calling, and Jesus emerged from the wilderness victorious. In the same way, God has been faithful to me throughout the forty years waiting for an answered prayer. His timing may not have matched mine, but His promises are always true. The answer to my prayer is a testament to His faithfulness and love for me.

Today, we still ascribe importance to forty days and forty nights. In Christianity, the period between Ash Wednesday and Easter is forty days (excluding Sundays). Lent is a time of holiness, when Christians remember the sacrifice of Christ and explore their own continuing process of sanctification, or becoming more Christ-like. Some give up a bad habit or take on a positive new practice during these forty days. It's our way today of honoring and modeling the clear significance of forty days and nights in the Bible and specifically the time Jesus spent fasting and enduring temptation in the desert.

Forty is an interesting number. The word "quarantine" is said to derive from it, specifically the Italian word *quarantina*, and the Centers for Disease Control note that in old times, ships arriving in Venice from infected ports were required to sit at anchor for forty days before landing. This would presumably give diseases time to die off.

Forty is also the typical number of weeks a woman is pregnant before she gives birth to a child.

But its religious significance is its most important. Today, we should consider whether God wants us to use a period of forty days and nights to learn a crucial lesson, end a negative practice, or adopt a new way of walking closer with Him.

My forty-year journey is a beautiful reflection of God's work in my life. While the wait may have felt long and arduous, it has also been a season of growth, refinement, and deepening faith. Just as the biblical stories of forty-year periods often led to profound breakthroughs, my life and perseverance is now being rewarded with the fulfillment of my childhood prayer.

After years of patience and spiritually treading water, I'm finally seeing the answer to my childhood prayers, and this has led to seeing the world with the fresh, hopeful eyes of a child again. My life has completely changed—it's as if I was once a caterpillar but after going through a near-death experience I've emerged as a butterfly!

While I initially saw my near-death experience as the answer to my prayers, it's more about the relationship I've built with Jesus. It's about the faith that has been tested and proven genuine. I now have more than just hope. Jesus revealed Himself to me in a very real way. I know for a fact that Jesus is real. He's a real person, as well as a very real God! My story is also a reminder that God's timing is perfect, even when it doesn't align with our expectations.

❖ ❖ ❖

As I step into this new season, I look back on the forty years prior to my NDE with gratitude for how God has shaped me. And I look forward with anticipation, knowing that the same God who has been faithful to me for four decades will continue to guide and bless me in the years to come. I am often reminded of the Bible verse found in Philippians 1:6: "…being confident of this, that he who began a good work in you will carry it on to completion until the day of Christ Jesus."

My story and yours are a powerful reminder that God's promises are worth waiting for and His timing is always worth trusting.

CHAPTER 15
A WORD TO THE NAYSAYERS

I've shared my story publicly for many years now. I have heard every excuse from people who refuse to believe me when I tell my story—that it wasn't an actual near-death experience. In my humble opinion most of the naysayers don't believe me because they simply don't believe in life after death. I've heard that my experience was caused by the drugs given to me during surgery, or it was just a reaction that everyone has when their brain is dying, or it was a hallucination from the high fever. I want to address each one of these. I believe that the research is and will continue to slowly lead us to the realization that NDEs are real. They are spiritual and hard to prove with modern science, but science is coming around.

Imagine going back fifty years and telling people that in the future, we could trace someone's family history or solve crimes by analyzing just a single strand of hair or a tiny drop of bodily fluid. They would have laughed at the idea, thinking it was impossible or science fiction. Yet, here we are today, where such advancements are not only real but commonplace.

This is similar to how many people view NDEs, right now. They dismiss them as unbelievable or unscientific, just like people in the past might have dismissed the idea of DNA analysis. But just as technology has proven the impossible to be possible, NDEs are increasingly being studied and understood in ways that challenge our assumptions about life, death, and consciousness. What seems unbelievable today might one day be widely accepted as truth.

❖ ❖ ❖

The first written account of a near-death experience is believed to come from Plato in 380 BC. The story is called the "Myth of Er." Don't let the term "myth" fool you. In Plato's day the word myth simply meant "word speech account" rather than the modern meaning. Plato tells of a soldier named Er who died in battle. He lay on the ground for ten days, then another two days on the funeral pyre; he awoke just before they lit it on fire. He sat up and told everyone about his journey to the afterlife. That had to be a wild scene!

❖ ❖ ❖

Dr. Peter Fenwick, a distinguished neuropsychiatrist and a leading expert on NDEs, has spent decades exploring the enigmatic relationship between the brain, consciousness, and the possibility that the mind might exist independently of the physical body. His work has challenged conventional scientific paradigms, inviting us to reconsider what it means to be conscious and whether consciousness is merely a product of the brain or something more profound.

Born in 1935, Fenwick trained as a psychiatrist and neuropsychiatrist, establishing a reputation for his rigorous scientific approach. However, his interest in the mysteries of consciousness led him to investigate phenomena that many in the scientific community dismissed as pseudoscience. In the 1970s, he began studying near-death experiences reports from individuals who, after being clinically dead or close to death, described vivid experiences such as floating outside their bodies, moving through tunnels of light, or encountering deceased loved ones.

Fenwick's research into NDEs revealed patterns that defied conventional explanations. Many patients reported detailed, lucid experiences during periods when their brains showed no measurable activity. These accounts often included verifiable details, such as conversations or events that occurred in other rooms that the patients could not have known through ordinary means. Fenwick began to question whether consciousness could exist independently of the brain, a notion that contradicted the prevailing materialist view that the mind is simply an emergent property of neural activity.

Dr. Fenwick proposed that the brain might act more like a filter or receiver for consciousness, rather than being its sole generator. He drew parallels to a television set: Just as a TV receives signals but does not create the broadcast, the brain might mediate consciousness without being its source. This idea, while controversial, offered a potential explanation for the vivid, coherent experiences reported by NDE survivors, even in the absence of brain activity.

Throughout his career, Fenwick collaborated with other researchers, including his wife, Elizabeth Fenwick, to document and analyze thousands of NDE cases. His work emphasized the transformative impact of these experiences, noting that many individuals returned with a profound sense of purpose, reduced fear of death, and increased compassion for others. These changes, he argued, were difficult to explain solely in terms of brain chemistry or psychological trauma.

Fenwick's exploration of consciousness extended beyond NDEs. He also studied end-of-life phenomena, such as deathbed visions, where dying individuals reported seeing deceased loved ones or other spiritual beings. These visions often brought comfort and peace to the dying, further suggesting that consciousness might transcend the physical body.

Despite facing skepticism from some quarters of the scientific community, Fenwick remained committed to his research, advocating for an open-minded, interdisciplinary approach to understanding consciousness. He believed that science should not shy away from exploring phenomena that challenge existing frameworks as they might hold the key to deeper truths about the nature of existence.

Dr. Peter Fenwick's work continues to inspire researchers and laypeople alike, encouraging us to consider the possibility that consciousness is more than a mere byproduct of the brain. His legacy is a testament to the power of curiosity and the importance of questioning the boundaries of what we think we know. Whether or not his theories are ultimately proven, Fenwick's contributions have expanded the conversation about life, death, and the mysteries of the mind, leaving an indelible mark on the fields of neuroscience and consciousness studies.

After devoting his life to studying near-death experiences he came to the conclusion that "There is no death. There is death of the body, but no death of the individual person." He went on to say, "I don't fear death at all. I'm looking forward to it." I would like to thank Dr. Fenwick for agreeing with the Holy Bible.

❖ ❖ ❖

Then there is the interesting story of Dr. Rajiv Parti. Dr. Rajiv Parti, a highly respected chief anesthesiologist at Bakersfield Heart Hospital in California, was known for his precision, expertise, and dedication to his patients. For years, he approached his work with a strictly scientific mindset, firmly rooted in the materialist view that consciousness was a product of brain activity. However, two profound experiences, one involving a patient and another his own near-death experience, would forever change his understanding of life, death, and the nature of consciousness.

One of the most striking cases in Dr. Parti's career involved a patient undergoing a complex surgical procedure. During the surgery, the patient's blood was completely replaced and the EKG machine showed a flatline, indicating no detectable brain activity. By all medical standards, the patient was clinically dead. Yet, after the surgery, the patient awoke and described the procedure in astonishing detail, including conversations between the surgical team and specific actions taken during the operation. The patient even recounted events that occurred in the operating room while they were seemingly unconscious and unresponsive. This experience left Dr. Parti deeply unsettled. How could someone with no measurable brain activity have such a vivid and accurate recollection of the surgery? It was a question that lingered in his mind, challenging his scientific training and beliefs.

Years later, Dr. Parti faced a life-threatening health crisis of his own. Diagnosed with advanced cancer, he underwent a series of grueling treatments, including surgeries and chemotherapy. During one of these procedures, he experienced a profound near-death experience that would transform his life. As his body struggled, Dr. Parti found himself floating above the operating table, observing the medical team working on him. He felt a sense of peace and detachment from his physical body, followed by a journey through a tunnel of light. He encountered spiritual beings who showed him a life review, where he was confronted with the consequences of his actions and the impact he had on others. The experience was vivid, lucid, and deeply transformative.

When Dr. Parti recovered, he was a changed man. The NDE had shattered his materialist worldview and convinced him that consciousness exists independently of the brain. He became a believer in the spiritual dimensions of life and death, a stark contrast to his previous skepticism. Dr. Parti began to share his experience publicly, writing about it in his book, *Dying to Wake Up: A Doctor's Voyage into the Afterlife and the Wisdom He Brought Back*. He described how his NDE had given him a new sense of purpose: to live a life of compassion, humility, and service to others.

Dr. Parti's journey from a skeptical anesthesiologist to a believer in the afterlife has inspired many, both within and outside the medical community. His story underscores the profound mystery of consciousness and the possibility that life extends beyond the physical body. Today, he continues to advocate for a deeper understanding of near-death experiences, bridging the gap between science and spirituality and encouraging others to consider the profound implications of these extraordinary phenomena.

There are several other prominent doctors and medical professionals who were initially skeptical of near-death experiences but became believers after experiencing one themselves. These individuals often describe their NDEs as life-changing events that profoundly altered their understanding of consciousness, the mind, and the possibility of life after death. Here are a few notable examples.

❖ ❖ ❖

Dr. Eben Alexander, a neurosurgeon with over twenty-five years of experience, was a staunch materialist who believed that consciousness was entirely a product of brain activity. He dismissed NDEs as hallucinations or illusions created by a dying brain. However, in 2008, his perspective changed dramatically when he contracted a rare form of bacterial meningitis that left him in a coma for seven days. During this time, his brain was so severely damaged that his doctors considered his chances of survival minimal.

While in the coma, Dr. Alexander experienced a vivid NDE in which he felt himself traveling through a mystical realm, encountering a beautiful, loving presence, and receiving profound spiritual insights. When he miraculously recovered, he was stunned to recall the experience in extraordinary detail, despite the fact that his brain had been nonfunctional during the event. This led him to conclude that consciousness exists independently of the brain. He later wrote about his experience in the bestselling book *Proof of Heaven: A Neurosurgeon's Journey into the Afterlife.*

❖ ❖ ❖

Dr. Mary Neal, an orthopedic surgeon, was another skeptic of NDEs until she experienced one herself. In 1999, while kayaking in Chile, she was trapped underwater for nearly fifteen minutes after a tragic accident. During this time, she was clinically dead. She described leaving her body, moving through a tunnel of light, and encountering spiritual beings who communicated with her. She was also shown glimpses of her future, including the death of her son, which later came true.

Before her NDE, Dr. Neal had been a scientifically minded individual who dismissed spiritual phenomena. However, her experience convinced her that consciousness survives physical death and that there is a spiritual dimension to existence. She has since written about her journey in *To Heaven and Back: A Doctor's Extraordinary Account of Her Death, Heaven, Angels, and Life Again.*

❖ ❖ ❖

Dr. Tony Cicoria, an orthopedic surgeon, was not a believer in NDEs or spirituality until he was struck by lightning in 1994. The incident left him clinically dead for several minutes. During this time, he experienced an out-of-body journey where he felt himself floating above his body, observing the scene below. He also encountered a bright light and felt an overwhelming sense of peace and love.

After his recovery, Dr. Cicoria became deeply interested in the nature of consciousness and the possibility of life after death. His experience led him to explore the spiritual dimensions of life, something he had never considered before.

✤ ✤ ✤

Dr. Bruce Greyson, a psychiatrist and NDE researcher, did not have an NDE himself, but his journey is worth noting. Initially a skeptic, he began studying NDEs after a patient described a vivid experience that defied medical explanation. Over decades of research, he became one of the world's leading experts on NDEs and a strong advocate for the idea that consciousness may exist independently of the brain. His work has helped bridge the gap between science and spirituality.

✤ ✤ ✤

The experiences of these doctors highlight a common theme: Many medical professionals who were once skeptical of NDEs became believers after experiencing or studying them. Their stories challenge the materialist view that consciousness is solely a product of brain activity and suggest that there may be more to existence than what science currently understands. These accounts also provide comfort to those who wonder about the nature of life, death, and what lies beyond.

While I am not a doctor, my near-death experience radically changed me too. And like the doctors I've mentioned, I was not a believer in such things. I was always curious about Heaven and longed to see it and have the proof that my limited mind is capable of. I remained a skeptic until it happened to me.

✤ ✤ ✤

So let's talk about my near-death experience. As I share this with you, I'm going to include a few comments I have received on social media and then explain why each one just doesn't add up.

First up is the idea that drugs caused my vision. Here are some comments related to that theory:

"Probably the anesthesia causing your brain to hallucinate."

"Propofol is intense stuff."

"Sounds like a trip on drugs from the OR."

"Is he not going to talk about him being under anesthesia prior to surgery?"

"Sounds cool but perhaps it was the drugs they gave him that caused these dream-like states?"

"The anesthesia is strong and can cause hallucinations, nothing more!"

"One could argue that the medicines were making him hallucinate, others will believe his story. I choose to believe, as there is no risk if I am wrong. I have everything to lose if it's real and I choose not to see it. God is real and Jesus is the way!"

I have to be honest; the last comment I listed sounds like "fire insurance" as we call it. I don't think salvation works like that, but God knows this person's heart.

Here are a few things to consider:

First, when Jesus walked into the surgical room, no drugs had been administered at all. At that point I had an IV in my hand and had been given fluids but no medication. Due to a medical condition, I require advance information about the specific medications that will be administered to me prior to surgery. I asked what I was being given and I was told it was just saline and electrolytes. "You can't have the good stuff yet," the nurse joked. Also, Jesus walked into the surgical room prior to the anesthesia mask being placed on my face.

And if drugs caused this so-called dream, then why did I have such complete recall? I was administered Versed, a medication commonly used during surgical procedures to induce temporary amnesia, preventing patients from recalling the experience. But I remembered everything in vivid detail.

And it wasn't just recalling the series of events. I could remember everything, including how I felt during my time in Heaven. I remembered how the skin on Jesus's hand felt. I remembered the sound and the warm feeling of the light beam going through my forehead. I remembered the feeling of the grass and how I was able to know the exact number of blades! I remembered the feeling of a warm breeze without feeling any wind. That memory is probably the hardest one to explain. There just aren't words to describe it. And I remember in vivid detail the colors of the sky. I just don't think it's possible to remember such details if this wasn't reality.

❖ ❖ ❖

Secondly, several people have told me that my high fever caused a hallucination. Let me share a few of those comments:

"What is going on is you had a 104 temperature and were hallucinating."

"Hallucinations. Pretty common when people are ill."

"It's called a hallucination. Very common with high fevers, etc."

While fever can, and in some cases does, cause hallucinations, mine was different. I've never heard of a hallucination you can interact with and touch and, when touched, that hallucination actually transports you to another place with physical, or should I say, beyond physical characteristics! Characteristics with heightened reality! And if my high fever caused a hallucination, what could possibly explain the next day when Jesus showed up again? I talked to Him for three hours! When He started talking, my fever was extremely high, but He talked for so long that my fever broke. He was still speaking when the nurse took my temperature and it was down to 100.5! That completely disproves the high fever hallucinations theory!

❖ ❖ ❖

The dying brain is another theory I hear quite often. Let's look at a few of my favorite "dying brain" comments:

"Hallucinations are not uncommon, they happen fairly frequently in or after very stressed conditions! People just aren't acquainted with them that much so their imagination does the rest, and they

'see things', also hear things, even feel things like someone touching them that are simply a product of mental stimulation or of an overactive imagination. Often these mental meanderings have to do with what they believe in, Jesus or God or angels picking up on the religious beliefs, suppositions or superstitions! The brain is a very complex organ that stores memories our whole lives. Some of them can be evoked at times more than others, but they are there in a certain part of our brain for as long as we live and certain situations can bring those memories to the forefront purposefully or not depending on the circumstances at the time!"

"Sadly, it's all hallucinogenic. It's caused by lack of oxygen to the brain. The brain is a wonderful organ; however, it's also a liar and a great soother at times of deep, deep stress. It helps us make death bearable."

"NDEs are nothing more than delusions generated by an oxygen starved brain. Amazing to see how detached people are from reality."

"If you research the effects of taking the drug DMT, this is so similar. DMT is a natural chemical released in your brain when you dream and when you die. Smoking it gives people this exact same experience."

"This happened because our brains fear death. Chemical reaction."

Let me take a minute to talk about DMT. This chemical is brought up quite often in most of the "dying brain theory" comments. It's a little scientific, so let me encourage you to read this section slowly. Frankly, it's a bit over my pay grade, but it's necessary to refute a very common argument against almost every NDE I've ever heard about.

No one has yet managed to identify the source or function of endogenous DMT, meaning DMT produced within the body. Scientists theorize that the pineal gland is the source of the body's DMT. The theory goes on to explain that the brain releases large amounts of the compound when we dream and during death, which would explain the profound imagery we experience when we sleep and supposedly when we enter a near-death episode or the dying process. Notice in the comments I listed above that the DMT theory is always presented as a fact when, in fact, it is only a theory. You see that quite often in social media comments.

Dr. David Nichols, pharmacologist and medicinal chemist, explains that the primary role of the pineal gland is to secrete melanin in order to regulate our sleep cycles. He goes on to explain that we are yet to uncover *any* evidence of DMT actually being produced in the pineal gland of humans. Furthermore, the quantity of DMT found in our blood is nowhere near enough to actually produce any effect when binding to sigma one receptors, which means that any claims about the compound playing a role and keeping cells alive or providing us with a mortal psychedelic send-off are at this stage nothing more than mere conjecture.

If my experience were something recalled by my dying brain, wouldn't I recall things that are familiar to me? I never could have anticipated that the Jesus I encountered would appear as He did. He looked very different from any picture of Him I had ever seen. As a kid, I was always shown pictures of Jesus as a blond-haired, blue-eyed man. That was completely different from the Jesus I met. If my dying brain was trying to comfort me, it wasn't doing a very good job! And the light beams from the Glory of the Lord? Where did that come from? It was the most amazing thing I have ever seen. Believe me when I tell you, I could never have imagined that in my wildest dreams!

Finally, consider the timing of it all. When Jesus told me, "It's the Glory of the Lord," my knees hit the ground and it was at that exact moment that I was shocked back to life.

❖ ❖ ❖

I've looked at all of these ideas through the years and I'm not convinced. I will say this, however. If this was somehow a dream, vision, or hallucination caused by fever, could that be used by God? I think the answer is pretty obvious and in fact is stated in the Bible in Romans 8:28: And we know that in all things God works for the good of those who love him, who have been called according to his purpose. But I believe wholeheartedly that Jesus answered my childhood prayers and took me to Heaven and showed me the glory of the Lord.

Many people don't know that before I had my NDE, I didn't believe in them completely. I had heard of them, but most of them I couldn't really explain. I am the kind of person who needs proof before I believe. I need to take apart a watch to see the gears and the springs to know how it works.

❖ ❖ ❖

There is one other theory that I must address. That is the theory put forth, mostly by my Christian brothers and sisters, that what happened to me is not biblical. I'll share some of those comments:

"Hebrews 9:27: 'Just as man is appointed to die once and after that to face judgment'. John 1:18: 'No one has ever seen God, but the one and only son who is himself God and is at the Father's side has made him known.' Folks need to have some DISCERNMENT when these types of stories show up. More times than not, they are earning $$$ from YouTube (per likes and subscribers), selling a book or making a paid appearance somewhere. Follow the money."

"Flesh and blood cannot inherit the kingdom of Heaven. Therefore, you cannot be with the Lord until he returns at the resur-rection. First Corinthians 15:52 through 53: in a moment in the twinkling of an eye, at the last trumpet for the trumpet shell sound, and the dead shall be raised [incorruptible], and we shall be changed. For this corruptible must put on incorruption, and this mortal must put on immortality. Until then you cannot be with the Lord, you must be changed. Only two people went to be with the Lord. Enoch in Elijah and some scholars believe Moses also. Common

sense, if we died and went to be with the Lord there would be no need for a resurrection and there would be no need to be changed. Sorry, but you're dead wrong."

"L O L, people actually believe these mind trick hallucinations to be real when biblically speaking it's impossible. Even Lazarus had no recollection. He was even dead for three days and when he came to, he never said where he was or what he saw. Ecclesiastes 9:5: for the living know that they shall die, but the dead note, not anything, neither have any more a reward for the memory of them is forgotten."

"All wrong. When you're dead, you're forever according to Holy Scripture. Isaiah 26:14: they are dead they shall not live. They are deceased. They shall not rise therefore hast thou visited and destroyed them and made all their memory to perish. Ecclesiastes 9:56: for the living know that they shall die, but the dead know neither have they anymore. A reward for the memory of them is forgotten. Also, their love and their hatred and their envy is now perished. Neither have any abortion for anything that is done under the sun. Ecclesiastes 1:27: then shall the dust return to the earth as it was, and the spirit shall return unto God who gave it. You were drugged up and hallucinating."

"Everybody please listen to me. We all want to believe these stories. Jesus tells us in Scripture, John 3:13: no one has ascended to heaven, but he that came down from heaven that is the son of man who is in heaven. We can't get to heaven until the resurrection! Our bodies will meet with our spirit and soul then we go to heaven. Enoch and Elijah are the only two who were taken to be with God. All the stories seem real to the person experiencing it. People love to hear stories like this. It reassures them. Don't put your faith in the stories. Listen to what Jesus said!"

Notice how there are no comments about the apostle Paul and his experience where he describes going to the third Heaven, whether in body or spirit? How could so many Christians be led astray and think I am not being truthful when everything I witnessed is biblical?

Could John have had a near-death experience on the island of Patmos when he received his vision from God, which led to his writing Revelation? Could Jacob's vision of a ladder, as found in Genesis 28:10, be a near-death experience? Throughout the Bible, God speaks to many people through visions. Why would He stop communicating this way once the Bible was written?

For Christians, the Bible is the inspired Word of God, a sacred text that reveals His character, His will, and His redemptive plan for humanity. It is a source of truth, guidance, and spiritual nourishment. However, the way we approach the Bible matters deeply.

Many people regularly take Bible verses out of context to make a point. Reading Scripture in context is not merely a scholarly exercise; it is a spiritual discipline that honors the integrity of God's Word and protects us from misinterpretation and misuse. Taking a single verse out of context, while often done unintentionally, can lead to misunderstanding, misapplication, and even harm. I believe this is a tactic of the enemy.

The Bible is not a collection of isolated verses or random thoughts; it is a unified narrative that tells the story of God's relationship with humanity. From Genesis to Revelation, the Bible reveals a coherent message of creation, fall, redemption, and restoration. Each book, chapter, and verse contributes to this grand narrative. When we read a verse in isolation, we risk divorcing it from the larger story, losing sight of its intended meaning and purpose.

For example, Jeremiah 29:11 is often quoted as a personal promise of prosperity: "For I know the plans I have for you, declares the Lord, plans to prosper you and not to harm you, plans to give you hope and a future." While this verse is comforting, it was originally spoken to the nation of Israel during their exile in Babylon. It was a promise of God's faithfulness to His covenant people, not a blanket guarantee of individual success. By understanding the historical and literary context we can appreciate the verse's true significance and apply it appropriately to our lives.

The practice of using isolated verses to support a particular belief or agenda is referred to as proof-texting. It is a common but dangerous approach to Scripture. It can lead to distorted theology and misguided practices.

For instance, Philippians 4:13, "I can do all things through Christ who strengthens me," is often cited to suggest that Christians can achieve any goal or overcome any obstacle. While this verse does emphasize Christ's empowering presence, its immediate context is Paul's contentment in all circumstances, whether in abundance or need. Taking it out of context risks turning it into a slogan for self-reliance rather than a declaration of dependence on Christ.

Similarly, Matthew 7:1, "Do not judge, or you too will be judged," is frequently used to discourage any form of discernment or accountability. However, when read in context, Jesus is warning against hypocritical judgment, not prohibiting all forms of evaluation. Later in the same chapter, He instructs His followers to discern false prophets by their fruits (Matthew 7:15–20). Ignoring this context can lead to a passive acceptance of sin and error, contrary to the Bible's call for holiness and truth.

Understanding the historical and literary context of a passage is essential for accurate interpretation. The Bible was written over thousands of years, in diverse cultures and languages and in various literary genres, including poetry, prophecy, history, and epistles. Each book reflects the circumstances and concerns of its original audience. For example, the Psalms were written as songs and prayers, expressing a range of emotions and experiences. Reading them as legal or doctrinal statements misses their poetic and devotional nature.

Likewise, the letters of Paul were addressed to specific churches facing particular issues. For instance, 1 Corinthians 11:6, which discusses head coverings for women, must be understood in light of the cultural norms of first-century Corinth. While the underlying principles of modesty and respect remain relevant, the specific application may differ in modern contexts. By studying the historical and cultural background we can discern the timeless truths of Scripture while avoiding out-of-date interpretations.

Reading the Bible in context requires humility, diligence, and reliance on the Holy Spirit. The Spirit, who inspired the Scriptures (2 Timothy 3:16), guides believers into all truth (John 16:13); however, the Holy Spirit's guidance does not negate the need for careful study and common understanding. The early church devoted itself to the apostles' teaching (Acts 2:42), and Christians today are called to study Scripture together, learning from one another and from the wisdom of the global Church throughout history.

Engaging with trusted commentaries, Bible study tools, and the insights of fellow believers can help us avoid personal biases and misinterpretations. As Proverbs 11:14 reminds us, "For lack of guidance, a nation falls, but victory is won through many advisors."

Reading the Bible in context is not just an academic exercise; it is an act of love and reverence for God's Word. It protects us from error, deepens our understanding, and enables us to apply Scripture faithfully in our lives. As Psalm 119:105 declares, "Your word is a lamp to my feet and a light to my path." To walk in its light, we must read it carefully, prayerfully, and in its entirety.

Let us, therefore, commit to a faithful and contextual reading of Scripture, trusting that the Holy Spirit will illuminate its truths and transform our hearts. In doing so, we honor God, grow in wisdom, and bear witness to the life-changing power of His Word.

Hank Hanegraaff, known as the "Bible Answer Man," emphasizes the importance of interpreting Scripture within the context of the entire Bible. He stresses the importance by following a few simple rules, including, "Avoid isolated readings of verses," one that I have already alluded to. He also promotes a method where clearer passages illuminate more ambiguous ones, which aligns with the biblical principle of analogy of faith, found in Romans 12:6. And finally, avoid cherry picking. In other words, don't select verses to fit preconceived ideas. I think he sums it all up nicely by advising everyone to, "Read Scripture in light of Scripture."

❖ ❖ ❖

I don't get comments like this very often, but here you go. I don't quite understand people like this. I hate to sound blunt, but the historical evidence of Jesus is easy to find.

"Jesus was made up to control the masses. He wasn't even real. Please, do some research before spewing your religion and lies."

"Dude, stop lying about a made up God. The Bible is a lie."

"As soon as I heard him say Jesus I turned it off. Jesus is a myth."

The historical evidence for Jesus of Nazareth outside of the Christian Bible comes from a variety of sources, including Roman, Jewish, and other early writings. While the number of specific historical documents that mention Jesus is relatively small, these references are significant because they come from non-Christian sources and provide external corroboration of His existence and impact. Here are the most notable historical documents and figures that mention Jesus:

- The first non-Christian author to mention Jesus is thought to be the Jewish historian Flavius Josephus, who wrote a history of Judaism in about the year 93, the famous *Antiquities of the Jews*. In his writings he mentions a number of figures from the New Testament, including Jesus, John the Baptist, and Jesus's "brother" James.

  In the *Antiquities*, Josephus writes, "There was about this time Jesus, a wise man, if it be lawful to call him a man, for he was a doer of wonderful works—a teacher of such men as receive the truth with pleasure. He drew over to him both many of the Jews, and many of the Gentiles. He was Christ; and when Pilate, at the suggestion of the principal men amongst us, had condemned him to the cross, those that loved him at the first did not forsake him, for he appeared to them alive again the third day, as the divine prophets had foretold these and ten thousand other wonderful things concerning him; and the tribe of Christians, so named from him, are not extinct at this day."

- The Roman historian Tacitus wrote about Jesus in his Annals (Book 15, Chapter 44), referencing the execution of Jesus under Pontius Pilate and the persecution of Christians in Rome during the reign of Emperor Nero.

- In a letter to Emperor Trajan, Pliny the Younger mentions Christians who worshipped Christ "as to a god." Here he is, summing up what he learned after interrogating Christians:

  "They were in the habit of meeting on a certain fixed day before it was light, when they sang in alternate verses a hymn to Christ, as to a god, and bound themselves by a solemn oath, not to any wicked deeds, but never to commit any fraud, theft or adultery, never to falsify their word, nor deny a trust when they should be called upon to deliver it up; after which it was their custom to separate, and then reassemble to partake of food, but of an ordinary and innocent kind."

- In *The Lives of the Caesars*, Suetonius refers to disturbances among the Jews instigated by "Chrestus," which many scholars interpret as a reference to Christ and early Christian activity in Rome.

- A Jewish historian, Josephus, mentions Jesus twice in his *Antiquities of the Jews*. The most famous passage, known as the "Testimonium Flavianum" (Book 18, Chapter 3), describes Jesus as a wise man who performed surprising deeds and was condemned to death by Pilate. He wrote, "About this time there lived Jesus, a wise man, if indeed one ought to call him a man. For he was one who performed surprising deeds and was a teacher of such people as accept the truth gladly." While some scholars believe this passage was later edited by Christian scribes, most agree that it contains an authentic core.

- In the Talmud, Jewish rabbinic writings contain a few references to Jesus, though they are often polemical and written centuries after his death. These texts refer to him as "Yeshu" and criticize His teachings and followers.

While the number of direct historical references to Jesus is limited, the combined evidence from Roman, Jewish, and early Christian sources provides a compelling case for His existence. These documents, written by authors with no vested interest in promoting Christianity, confirm that Jesus was a historical figure who lived in first century Judea, gathered followers, and was executed under Pontius Pilate. The scarcity of references is not unusual for a figure from a remote province of the Roman Empire, and the impact of Jesus's life and teachings is evident in the rapid spread of Christianity in the centuries that followed.

❖ ❖ ❖

And I'll close this chapter with a few of my favorite comments. They warm my heart and put a smile on my face, and I believe they put a smile on the face of the King:

"Amazing testimony! God, the Holy One, we can't compare him to anyone. He lives forever. He created all the world. Praise the Lord."

"Yes, my life changed forever. I am totally in love with Jesus. I kept quiet for a while, then Jesus told me to tell my testimony. Real life experiences change people's lives."

"I enjoy and love this conversation, love Mike's story. Thank you for these programs, for intelligent discussion and explorations of people's experiences with God. It seems so well centered on genuine God experiences not wandering into other deceptive spiritual realms. Great stuff."

"God bless you my brother and thank you for sharing the beauty of our Lord and Savior Jesus Christ."

"Beautiful testimony."

One thing I have learned through the experience of sharing my near-death experience is that God was certainly preparing me. I believe every word He told me during my hospital stay was to prepare me for this task. It is not easy becoming a bold ambassador for Christ, but I am not doing this for any rewards here on Earth. I am doing this out of obedience to Him. Jesus called on me to fulfill my purpose. When I think about the calling on my life, several Bible passages come to mind. Philippians 2:13: "For it is God who works in you to will and to act in order to fulfill his good purpose." And, of course, probably one of the most fitting verses is found in Philippians 1: "...being confident of this, that he who began a good work in you will carry it on to completion until the day of Christ Jesus."

He asked and I am answering, maybe reluctantly at first, but it is worth it. I have grown in my faith and my security in knowing that Jesus is real and is the only way to the Father. Eternity is real. Heaven is real. I look forward to the day when I see Jesus face-to-face once again and He says, "Well done, good and faithful servant."

CHAPTER 16
WORDS OF ENCOURAGEMENT

A Christian testimony is a personal account of faith, often sharing how God has transformed your life. It is both a proclamation of belief and an act of obedience to Jesus's call to "make disciples" (Matthew 28:19). While we will never be able to see the full impact of our testimony here on Earth, God does at times give us a glimpse of our impact on His Kingdom.

The effects of sharing your faith, such as planting seeds of hope, inspiring repentance, or strengthening others, are often spiritual and may unfold over time. These outcomes are not always tangible or immediately observable. The Bible says in 1 Corinthians 3:6–7, "I planted, Apollos watered, but God gave the growth."

Like the parable of the sower found in Mark 4:26–29, growth can occur in secret. Someone may hear my testimony years later and respond unbeknownst to me.

Hebrews 11:1 defines faith as "the assurance of things hoped for, the conviction of things not seen." Trusting that God uses our testimonies, even when we don't witness results, aligns with this principle. It discourages seeking validation through visible "success," (even though that goes against our worldly instruction and instinct), instead encouraging faithfulness regardless of observable outcomes. 2 Corinthians 5:7 puts it this way: "We walk by faith, not by sight."

Yes, there are times when you as a Christian can lead someone to salvation through Jesus, but we do not save anyone. That is up to the Holy Spirit. Salvation is purposed by the Father, accomplished by the Son, and applied by the Holy Spirit. Without the Spirit's agency in salvation, all that Christ has accomplished brings no value to us.

As Scripture uniformly presents, the Spirit graciously, effectively, and permanently gives us Christ Jesus and every blessing He has secured. Our salvation is in Christ alone. Our salvation is by His Spirit alone.

❖ ❖ ❖

I had a very close friend, in fact my best friend, who was killed in an auto racing accident. He wasn't just my best friend; he was an outstanding guy and a true leader in our community. I was devastated. Our families vacationed together, we coached baseball together, and we shared the same core values. He was well known and loved. There were about 1,000 people at his funeral.

Part of the reason I was so devastated is that even though he and I spent so much time together, I wasn't sure he was a Christian and that bothered me a lot. My mission on Earth is to make sure my friends are going to be there in Heaven with me or at least talk to them about God. Sadly, we talked about everything worldly, everything except God.

The one time the subject of faith came up, he said, "I've got an aunt that's a nun. She will probably cover all of us." I just giggled.

"I don't know if it works that way," I replied.

I could have talked to him about faith in Jesus, but I didn't. The thing that keeps me going is that after he hit a wall going 100 mph, maybe he sat there for a few minutes or even a few seconds and God gave him a chance in that time to turn to Him.

When we die, I picture God asking us, "What did you do with my Son?"

Maybe he had a few minutes or a few seconds to say yes. He had never turned his back on Jesus or denied His existence to me, so I stayed hopeful. It has remained one of my greatest regrets. I should have taken that opportunity that God seemingly gave me to tell my friend about Him, about Jesus. After he died, I changed the way I interact with people and friends. When I get to know someone, I try to drill down and find out what their belief is.

Even so, I had the same reaction to his death that many people have who lose family members or friends. I was angry with God. Through that anguish, I came to realize several things that had a heavy impact on my life. I realized that his death wasn't caused by God. It was his choice to start racing cars after we stopped coaching baseball. He was an adrenaline junky and he loved taking risks and going fast! A few years before his death, we took our sons on a heart-stopping adventure—bungee jumping. I was scared to death to jump and had to inch my way off the platform. My friend was the first to go and did so in his familiar fearless style—he dove head first and couldn't wait to go again once his feet were back on the ground!

I also came to the stark realization that when you become a Christian you say no to you and yes to the Kingdom. Whatever is best for the Kingdom, you agree to. That's why Jesus said we should pray: "Let your Kingdom come and your will be done on Earth as it is in Heaven."

I think that is what it means to die to yourself. Finally, I conceded that if something good comes from my friend's death, then it's worth it. But what good could come from such a terrible loss?

Five years after his death, I ran into another friend of mine on a softball field. This friend told me that he became a Christian after attending the funeral of our mutual friend. In fact, he is now one of those "on fire" Christians and has raised his kids that way.

He said, "I thought I was a Christian before, but maybe not. I left the funeral and got saved and baptized. Death can happen to anybody and I know I can die at any time. I had to get right with the Lord."

Back to the Lord's Prayer. "Let your Kingdom come and your will be done on Earth as it is in Heaven."

God's kindness still takes my breath away. In the middle of that crushing pain, He let me see a flicker of His plan, something good, something lasting, rising from the ashes. I'll never stop thanking God for this. Part of me will always wonder where the ripples of our suffering may land, who they will reach, and how He might weave them into the tapestry of His glory. I've made peace with the idea that I may never know—at least not this side of eternity. Yet I rest in this: I know the author of my story, and that is enough.

We were made to live forever, something I can't possibly comprehend now. But one day, we will finally glimpse the span of our days on earth as God does.

CLOSING PRAYER

Heavenly Father,

Thank you for your faithfulness throughout my life and especially in the forty-year waiting period where you shaped and molded my mind, body and spirit to conform with your will. Thank you for your faithfulness and patience and for walking with me through every moment of waiting, testing, and preparation. As I now see the fulfillment of a lifelong prayer, may everyone I encounter in my journey feel your presence and love more deeply than ever before. I pray you help them to trust in your perfect timing and to use this experience as a testimony of your goodness. May every new season be filled with joy, purpose, and a deeper connection with you. In Jesus's name, Amen.

ONE LAST NOTE

Yes, it finally happened—I nailed that elusive hole in one on February 13, 2009! Melissa and I were playing Mountain Springs Golf Club in Sonora, California, a stunning golf course in the foothills, and the magic unfolded on hole twelve, a challenging par three stretching 137 yards. I pulled out my trusty nine iron, took a deep breath, and let it fly. The ball soared through the air, landed on a slight hill about ten feet behind the pin, and then, thanks to some perfect backspin, it rolled back toward the hole like it had a mind of its own. And then... plunk! It dropped right in.

I couldn't believe it! I sprinted all the way to the green, heart pounding, and yanked the ball out of the hole like I'd just won the lottery. The celebration that followed was pure joy—jumping, shouting, and maybe even a little disbelief. It was a moment I'll never forget and one that still gives me goosebumps just thinking about it.

Mike McKinsey: Author, Speaker, and Beacon of Faith

ABOUT THE AUTHOR

Mike McKinsey is an accomplished author, real estate investor, and a passionate advocate for spreading the love of Jesus Christ. Residing in Chattanooga, Tennessee, Mike balances a fulfilling personal life with a thriving professional career. Married and blessed with thirteen grandchildren, he finds joy in family, storytelling, and the simple pleasures of life, including the companionship of two beloved dogs and a cat.

In 2004, Mike experienced a profound near-death experience (NDE) that forever changed his perspective on life, death, and the nature of existence. This transformative event inspired a deep curiosity about spirituality, consciousness, and the interconnectedness of all things. Drawing from this life-altering experience, Mike has woven themes of hope and resilience into his writing, offering readers a unique glimpse into the mysteries that lie beyond the physical world.

Mike continues to share his testimony and insights through his writing, inspiring others to embrace life's challenges with courage and to remain open to the profound possibilities that exist beyond the everyday. With a heart full of gratitude and a spirit of curiosity, he looks forward to continuing his journey of growth, discovery, and a deeper relationship with Christ.

Let's connect on social media.
Find my links at MikeMcKinsey.com.

For more great books from Peak View Press
Visit Books.GracePointPublishing.com

If you enjoyed reading *I Held the Hand of Jesus in Heaven,* and purchased it through an online retailer, please return to the site and write a review to help others find the book.

www.ingramcontent.com/pod-product-compliance
Lightning Source LLC
Chambersburg PA
CBHW071344090426
42738CB00012B/2999